TOYNBEE ON TOYNBEE

Toynbee on Toynbee

A Conversation between
Arnold J. Toynbee and G. R. Urban

New York
OXFORD UNIVERSITY PRESS
1974

Preface

This small book originated in a series of twelve radio discussions which Dr. Toynbee and I recorded for the 1972-73 programs of Radio Free Europe, with whose kind cooperation it is here published. The nature of the medium made for a brief, simple, and informal exposition; it limited the number of topics we could deal with and ruled out any correlative survey of the antecedents of particular arguments marshaled on this or that side of the conversation. Some of the critical points raised have been extensively covered in *Reconsiderations,* others are new to this volume. We attempted to pay about equal attention to Dr. Toynbee's method of historical enquiry and to the framework of history that emerged from it. The choice of problems selected for discussion within these two broad categories reveals a double bias: one emphasizing the history of communist countries and parties, and the other, linked by contrast to the first, concentrating the discussion on the numinous element in Dr. Toynbee's *A Study of History.* The first bias is explained by the context in which the conversation took place and my own interest in testing Dr. Toynbee's laws against East European affairs; the second has to do with my curiosity to see to what extent a unitary metaphysico-theological system of history is capable of replacing religious orthodoxies and stilling some of the anxiety of our time.

G. R. Urban

TOYNBEE ON TOYNBEE

approaches

URBAN Is history a science; is it an art; or is it a bit of both? Since Descartes and Vico, historians have been divided on this question: intellectual curiosity urges us to ask with Ranke *wie es eigentlich gewesen,** while emotions lead us to believe with Goethe *das Beste, was wir von der Geschichte haben ist der Enthusiasmus, den sie erregt.*† Perhaps we can find some answer to this problem by discussing the nature of historical facts — whether they differ from the kind of facts we find in a poem or in mathematics. The charge that the historian is arbitrary in the selection of his facts is as commonly made as the contrary accusation that he is a mere scissors-and-paste man — not a master of historical facts, but a chronicler of recorded events. If he is a pattern-maker his credentials as a scholar are questioned; the evolution of human society, Sir Karl Popper writes (echoing H. A. L. Fisher) "is a unique historical process. . . . Its description . . . is not a law, but only a singular historical statement." If he is a weaver of raw cloth, he is accused (as for instance by J. H. Plumb) of being one of "thousands of historians scurrying like ants over the debris of time, but often possessing no more than an ant's vision."

How then does an historian run his fact-detector over this debris of time? There is a passage in Sir Fred Hoyle's *Of Men and Galaxies* which challenges the historian to search for his facts with the kind of method in mind which the exact sciences have evolved:

Chance effects occur in science, and in all human activities. This, indeed, is one of the biggest problems the historian has to face up to, perhaps his biggest problem — to separate chance effects, *noise* as the physicist calls it, from systematic trends. I often suspect

* What actually happened.
† The most precious thing we have from history is the enthusiasm it inspires.

that some of my historical colleagues make the mistake of thinking it necessary to know everything about everything . . . no
serious attempt has been made to separate what is random from
what is systematic. There are, of course, obvious dangers in making such a separation. . . . But exactly the same problem occurs
in the sciences as well as in the humanities, and scientists have
evolved methods for dealing with it. . . . Serious arguments
about signal and noise hardly ever arise in physics. . . . [The
historian] is not quite sure what is important and what is trivial,
so everything has to go in.

TOYNBEE I suppose in both physical science and in the study of human
affairs the test of the difference between what is chance and
what is law — regularity — is one's conception of the structure of
non-human nature and the structure of human nature. There
must be some common element of regularity in human nature
as well as in physical nature. I think the difference is one of
degree: Obviously human nature is much subtler, there are
many more catches in it. Let me give two illustrations of what
I mean. In the study of human affairs the question of selecting what is significant, and what in the future may prove
significant, is very important. I am told that when the Public
Record Office was founded in this country it was over-
whelmed with masses of documents so that the people in
charge said they could not house all these documents, let
alone handle them. They thought they would have to destroy
an awful lot, and there was discussion about what they
should destroy. I am told they destroyed all the documents,
public and private, dealing with the building of the railroads
in England on the ground that this dull, pedestrian subject
could not possibly interest anyone. Today economists would
give anything to have those records. The point is that one
simply couldn't predict less than a century ago what would
now be regarded as of great importance. Another case: About
the time of Augustus, Greek students of literature decided
that fifth and fourth century Attic literature was the proper
standard and that people must try to write again in this Attic

form. They scrapped what lay between the original, classical Attic and their own pseudo-Attic. This was a case of applying pedantic, purely stylistic criteria to a subject where such criteria were not only inappropriate but positively damaging. Today we would give anything to have the lost literature between those two periods.

Another question that is relevant here is the question of death. This does not arise in the natural sciences, although atoms are constantly dying to be reborn, if I may speak figuratively, but they are doing so in such vast quantities that the disintegration and reconstruction of a particular atom is not significant, whereas in human affairs a particular person's duration of life may be very significant. Supposing Alexander the Great's father, Philip, had not been assassinated but had lived to his full natural expectation of life, Alexander wouldn't have had his career. Supposing Alexander, instead of dying of a sickness at the age of 33, had lived to the average age of his generals, who were rather long-lived — into his 70s or 80s — history would have been quite different.

The objective accident of death and the subjective difficulty of predicting what in the long run is going to seem significant to people make it extremely difficult for historians to distinguish signal from noise. Hoyle is quite right, and I can't see a solution to this problem.

URBAN The answer hasn't been found, and the uncertainty in which the historian works has made it rather easy for the dilettante and the man with an axe to grind to pass his stuff off for the genuine article. Nevertheless, historians do have a tacit yardstick: They talk of work that is intellectually honest, that is a good piece of research and craftsmanship; of history that is acceptable and history that is not. What sort of criteria do historians use when they make these distinctions? What do we mean when we say that the writings of Alfred Rosenberg or Stalin's *Short Course* are unacceptable because they lack intellectual integrity?

TOYNBEE Let's start with the deliberately biased histories. Rosenberg is a good example, but the historian's prejudice is usually more skillfully camouflaged. There are many historical conferences — not bona fide intellectual conferences but conferences with a political purpose behind them — where the disputes are masked as intellectual arguments. For instance, what, if any, contribution did the Scandinavians make to early Russian history? How far, in the sixth and seventh centuries A.D., did the Slavs swamp the Greeks — are the present-day Greeks largely descended from these Slavs, or are they virtually pure Greeks? Were the Rumanians in Hungary before the Magyars, or did they come in after the Magyars had established themselves in the Carpathian basin? All these problems are voluminously discussed on political-national lines. The person who is not politically engaged can readily discern the bias behind the arguments. Then — a more difficult case — some people believe they have the everlasting, assured truth about the universe. If you were a Jew and were studying the Christian interpretation of the Torah, you would be astonished and disgusted by the way in which the Christians have recklessly deformed the obvious original meaning of the Old Testament to make it all into a prophecy of Christianity. But if you look again at the Torah you will see that the Jews themselves — as higher criticism has brought out — distorted history to fit a Jewish monotheistic theory of history: the divine providence of the unique god Yahweh shaping the history of human affairs. Now, this particular shaping of the past to fit in with a higher religious philosophy is more respectable than Rosenberg, and therefore much more formidable —

URBAN — history being the victor's propaganda —

TOYNBEE — quite, and you cannot get to the bottom of these distortions. The archeologists have begun to rewrite the Biblical story to a certain extent from the Phoenicians' and Philistines' points of view. Although the Philistines' and Phoenicians' written works haven't survived, we are getting evidence of their material culture and their religious culture from the remains of temples, images, and so on. In Northern Syria, for example, at Ras-ash-shamrah, we have had tablets dug up dating back to the fourteenth century B.C. with a lot of Phoenician mythology on them. So partially, but only partially, the archeologists can recover the Phoenicians' and the Philistines' statements of their cases. What they can do is to show that the Bible has to be taken with a grain of salt, and that we must allow for the fact that the Jews got away with telling the tale. The picture of the Jews' relations with their neighbors has been inherited by Christians entirely from the Jewish point of view. Even Christians who have been hostile to Jews haven't been able to escape from this Jewish presentation of history. So the victor does have an enormous advantage, and one of the things the historian must be on his guard against is letting the victor monopolize the telling of the tale to posterity.

URBAN You seem to have been very conscious of the need of putting the case of the underdog in your personal life too. Philip Toynbee tells us how, after the First World War, you gave him an educational tour, so to speak, of Turkey and Germany because you felt that war propaganda had distorted the Englishman's picture of these countries and you didn't want your son to be brought up on so unbalanced a view.

TOYNBEE When the English were powerful in the nineteenth century they had their foreign pets who were generally so-called oppressed nationalities. For a time after 1848-49 the Magyars were the English Liberals' pets; then people like Seton-Watson saw that the Slovaks and Rumanians inside Hungary were not getting a fair deal from the Magyars, and *they* became the Englishmen's pets against the Magyars to the consternation of the Magyars. So this is probably a hangover of the lordly English people's liking to be patrons of oppressed peoples. A. J. P. Taylor's recent picture of Hitler (in *Origins of the Second World War*) is a late and extreme case — a *reductio ad absurdum* — of this attitude: as Hitler is in the doghouse, an Englishman gets up and defends him. If Hitler had won and founded his one-thousand-year Reich, Taylor would have found no use for him at all.

Now, a similar case to the Biblical story — of the dangers of adopting the victor's one-sided nomenclature — is ancient Greek history: It is written almost entirely from the Athenian point of view. Every modern historian writes about the so-called Peloponnesian War as seen from the Athenian point of view — the enemy are the Peloponnesians. We don't speak of the Atheno-Peloponnesian War, but, if the Spartans and Boeotians had written the story and this had survived, we should have a very different account. I've always been very conscious of the need to deflate the victor's propaganda. I wrote a biggish book on a bit of Roman history, called *Hannibal's Legacy,* because I became very conscious that the Romans not only wrote the history of their dealings with other people from the Roman point of view, but also imposed this on the modern world: We talk of the Punic Wars, not the Romano-Punic Wars, assuming that we are really Romans confronting Carthaginians. But if we had an account of these wars written by a Carthaginian historian, we should probably find Rome's Punic Wars being called "Carthage's 'Roman Wars.'" A double name of a war is the only kind that is duly neutral. We have evidence that there were histories of Rome's war with Carthage and Rome's transactions with Carthage written by Greek historians who were sympathetic to Carthage and not to Rome, and these are sometimes cited by Polybius, but it is no accident that these works have not survived and the pro-Roman Polybius has survived. It is no accident that there is no surviving Philistine or Phoenician account of the story in the Books of Kings in the Old Testament. Nevertheless, apart from archeology, we do have some evidence of the "nonestablishment" point of view, because both the Jews and the Athenians had an opposition party. The prophets are, so to speak, the internal critics of Jewish history, and men like Plato and Thucydides give one a glimpse of the internal disapproval, even condemnation, of Athenian democracy by some of the Athenians themselves. So, thanks to there being an opposition inside the victorious party, the tale as told by the victors, though they monopolize the story, isn't a completely self-consistent presentation of the Athenians and Jews being all the way virtuous and the enemy all the way bad. There is some counterevidence from inside.

It's the criterion of objectivity we are trying to find. As far as an historian is guided by disinterested curiosity, he is probably on safe ground, but then the curiosity itself is subjective, because we aren't omnivorously curious about everything. Any study of human affairs is bound to be selective. Supposing someone had in his hands all the newspapers published in the world on a single day and supposing he had a guarantee that every word reported was gospel truth. What could he do with those papers? How could he organize them? Supposing further that he thought that all the facts were of equal importance — he just couldn't produce a history of a single day incorporating all those facts. He'd have to select, and, even if he reproduced all the facts, he would have to star some and depress others. And the moment you do this you begin to become subjective. I'm conscious of the preferences and prejudices that come into play, but it is very hard for the writer to see them himself.

A fact in history is not really something concrete, like a brick or a stone, that you can pick up and handle; a fact is man-made in a sense — it is the result of a selection from the raw material. Even a brick is a *selection* from the world's clay. This is our difficulty. I think here historians have a lot to learn from physical scientists, because scientists are extremely honest about truth. They are ready ruthlessly to scrap their most cherished hypotheses if one single piece of evidence makes a hypothesis untenable. It's a point of honor with scientists. Now, *a fortiori*, historians ought to have this sense of honor: we ought always to be ready to think again, to discard the most cherished systems or selections of facts or attitudes toward so-called facts if further research calls for changes — not only because of the discovery or manufacture of new facts, but because of further reflection about existing so-called facts too.

This is very necessary.

URBAN What you are saying is that history is what historians write, not what actually happened, because it is only through the cognitive process of the historian that we can read meaning into an otherwise random accumulation of facts. Yet I can think of at least one respectable view which holds that the historian's truth is more real than the scientist's because it is independent from the artificiality of scientific experiments. This view is convincingly put by R. G. Elton, in *The Practice of History*, where he says, for example, that the treatment of cells for purposes of study in biochemistry, or even the dropping of a stone from the tower of Pisa, is artificial. "These things would not have happened," he says, "but for a deliberate act of will on the part of the experimenter; the matter studied may be taken from nature, but before it is studied it is transformed for the purposes of the investigation." Not so with history. The historian, Elton argues, although he may select his problems to suit himself, is nevertheless confronted with real facts — a dead reality which is independent of the enquiry. "Just because historical matter is in the past, is gone, irrevocable and unrepeatable, its objective reality is guaranteed: it is beyond being altered for any purpose whatsoever."

TOYNBEE The historian does select; he doesn't take information indiscriminately from the past but chooses those bits of information that seem to him significant and rejects others. This activity is, in fact, very similar to the scientist's artificial experiments. The similarity has to do with the working of the human mind which is common to all operations of the mind whether the intellect is studying human or non-human nature. It is, so to speak, processing the perception of phenomena — the scientist's facts and the historian's facts alike are processed by the mind before they can become what we call facts. So I don't agree with Elton.

URBAN Ideally we should aim, as you say, for the disinterested study of the past for its own sake. But as that is most unlikely to be achieved, you suggest in one of your books that the historian should "put his cards on the table." But are we to believe that the historian is capable of being conscious of his prejudices, and that he is humble enough to put them on public view? If that were possible, would he not attempt to write what would appear to him to be unprejudiced history in the first place? But supposing the historian is sufficiently self-critical and contrite to declare the goods he carries in his luggage, wouldn't he then be tempted to feel free from the constraints of disinterested enquiry and excuse himself by saying, with Acton, that the historian is, after all, a politician with his face turned backward? I am pressing this point because you are yourself often accused of having written a prophetic type of history, and although you have put your cards on the table, you are still apt to be misunderstood and misrepresented. So the integrity of the historian is no guarantee that we will know how to correct the picture he has painted for us — the caveat becomes, as it were, part of the message.

TOYNBEE Yes, the historian is likely to be unconscious of his most fundamental prejudices. These may be obvious to other people, but, for the historian himself, they are so implicitly taken for granted that it may be difficult for him to haul them up to the level of his consciousness and display them to himself and to his readers.

In general, I think there is bound to be an element of subjectivity and relativity in any study of human affairs. *Homo sum, humanum nihil a me alienum puto.* The spectator is also an actor. He is involved in the events that he is observing and recording. However remote in time and place the events in question may be, he is still involved because these are human events, and he himself is a human being. If the historian is honest, self-critical, and well versed in the art of introspection and psychological analysis, he will certainly do his best to write an unprejudiced history; but, even so, his success cannot, I believe, be more than partial.

I have quoted in my books the Italian philosopher Croce as saying that all history is contemporary history. What he means is that every human being is situated in a point-moment of time, and he can only observe the universe from this shifting point-moment in his very brief life. This is really relativity applied, as it should be, not only to non-human nature but to human affairs too. It is impossible for a human being to jump clear of his situation in time-space and to look at things from outside the universe and outside time with the eye of a hypothetical god. I remember Henri Frankfort criticizing me on a point that illustrates what I mean. I had apparently disparaged the ancient Egyptian civilization for being static. Frankfort said: Why on earth disparage it for that? Why isn't the Egyptian ideal of keeping society static just as good as your wretched modern, Western idea of dynamism? And when we look at the world today we see there is a great deal in what he said, and we are beginning to think we must stabilize our civilization. I quite agree that my view of history is colored by my experience in life. It has been stimulated by the experience of various good and bad things which happened in public affairs in my own lifetime, and I can't get away from that. I have always had a foot in writing recent, so-called contemporary history.

It is true that I am bona fide more interested in the history of some parts of the past than I am in the history of my own times. I am probably more interested in Greek and Roman history in the last millennium B.C. than in contemporary world history, and I enjoy studying the Greek and Roman and Islamic and Chinese Ts'in periods more than studying the modern, westernized world, which I don't much like. But I am a member of contemporary society, I have a stake in its survival, I have children, grandchildren and great-grandchildren whom I wish to see survive in a possible world, and I echo a noble thing Bertrand Russell is said to have said very late in his life: It is very important to care immensely about what is going to happen after you are dead. I think this is very right, but, from the point of view of trying to be an objective historian, this is probably a distorting element. How can we jump clear of our position in space-time? We aren't God — I don't know whether there is a God, but anyway, if there is, we can't be that.

URBAN Some of your critics accuse you precisely of taking an almost godlike view of history in the sense of bringing together and finding patterns in the study of civilizations, nations, classes, and races which are not — or are thought by them not to be —

strictly comparable. I suppose the frequent references to Polybius in your *Study* tell us something about the origins of your comprehensive view of history. I am thinking particularly of Book I, Chapter 4 of Polybius's *Oecumenical History* (which you quote in a footnote) where Polybius asks:

What should we say of somebody who visited the world's most famous cities one by one . . . and then immediately assumed that, by this process, he had acquired a knowledge of the physiognomy of the whole World, including its entire layout and structure? People who are convinced that historical specialization will give them a fairly good synoptic view of the whole of history are, it seems to me, suffering from a delusion. They remind me of people who have taken a look at the *disjecta membra* of an organism that was once alive and beautiful, and who then imagine that they have had a first-hand view of this creature in all its activity and beauty. . . . The truth is that the part may give us a genuine knowledge or an accurate appreciation of it. . . . A panoramic view . . . enables one to find utility as well as enjoyment in history.

Now, you seem to echo this view in a variety of very striking formulations. You say in one instance (quoting P. Bagby) that there is a case for looking at human affairs through the macroscope rather than the microscope. Then you talk of the different cultural configurations in which our common human nature has expressed itself, and you urge us not only to understand them and to appreciate them, but also to "love them as being parts of mankind's common treasure."

TOYNBEE Polybius had an enormous influence on me. I studied Greek and Roman history at Oxford, and I chose a period of Roman history in which one of the original sources you had to read was the relics of the work of Polybius. Polybius's theme is that, within a period of less than fifty-three years, Rome unified the entire civilized world — of course, he was not conscious of the Eastern half of the civilized world, but we see what he means: Rome unified the whole Mediterranean Basin. Now, this is a universal view of history which has interested me all my life.

Polybius was an exception among Greek historians in trying to take a view of the whole thing. He had a famous predecessor, Herodotus, but most Greek historians wrote about particular episodes — they wrote the history of a particular war, like Thucydides, or they wrote the history of some particularly famous soldier, philosopher or politician, like Plutarch.

This emphasis on particulars was in a sense paradoxical, because in theory Hellenic thinkers despised particulars as being unworthy of intellectual attention, and thought much more highly of generalities. Aristotle expresses this very clearly in his *Poetics* where he says that poetry is a higher thing than history precisely because it concerns itself with the universal, whereas history tends to express the particular. But, as I say, in Hellenistic times, as in the nineteenth and twentieth centuries in our own world, the characteristic way of writing history was episodic, and Polybius was consciously in opposition to this — he set out to correct it. He is polemical and very sharp in his criticism of these episodic historians. I have been conscious of the same thing myself, because if you approach human affairs through Greek and Latin language and literature, you cannot divide human affairs into history, architecture, art, literature, and so on. There is an inseparable unity in all these sides of civilization, and, owing to my classical education, this sense of a unity has influenced me all through my life.

I do feel that the family of which I am a member is the whole of mankind from the beginning to the still unreached end of its history. Though I am an Englishman born in A.D. 1889, I also feel my kinship with a hominid born 2 million years ago and with one who may be born 2000 million years after my death.

URBAN How did you first become conscious of regularities in history?

TOYNBEE I expected to be a Greek and Roman historian spending all my time and energy on Greek and Roman history. My first job was at Oxford where I was a so-called ancient history don — and I started by absorbing as much knowledge of my subject as I could. And when I had taken my degree I began to absorb what I hadn't studied as an undergraduate. I was teaching Greek and Roman history when the First World War broke out and it suddenly struck me, teaching people from Thucydides, that Thucydides had already anticipated our experiences, namely the outbreak of a great war, which he immediately saw as a turning point in the history of his civilization. *We* were just coming to that point, which meant that although Thucydides was centuries back in chronological time, measured by the experience of human affairs and destiny he had already experienced what I was just reaching, and this made me see that one could put Greek and Roman history side by side with modern Western history and compare them right outside the chronological framework. This rather sudden flash of insight made me realize that I must organize my study of history — not just amass more and more shapeless information — and that I must organize it on comparative lines. Next, I found that comparing Greek and Roman history with only modern Western history wouldn't do — I must compare all the histories of all civilizations and obtain enough information about each of them to make a reasonable comparative study of the gamut of them. The patterns and regularities which you find in my *Study* emerged empirically from these comparisons.

URBAN Some of your critics say that one cannot infer "laws" from the comparative study of civilizations — that history, unlike natural science, cannot be nomothetic because the particulars of historic studies are never numerous enough to permit generalizations. You speak, largely in terms of biological symbolism, of the birth, growth, breakdown, and disintegration of civilizations of which you identify twenty-one. Mightn't your critics be right in saying that this is too small a number?

If one examined the life histories of twenty-one human beings, one would probably find one or two born with some congenital imperfection inherited from distant ancestors. These lives would be short, uncreative, or creative in perhaps freak ways. Other lives would run into accidents early or in the middle of their normal span and be extinguished. Yet others would experience a sudden spurt of activity later, having shown no promise in youth, and there would be those — like mathematicians and musical prodigies — who showed early promise only to disappoint later in life. In other words, we would probably find human equivalents both of your four "abortive" and five "arrested" civilizations, leaving us with a sample of only twelve. Would we have reason to trust a doctor who generalized from only twelve case histories?

Obviously civilizations share certain characteristics because they are the work of human beings. But the question would still persist in a critic's mind whether generalizations of the kind you make wouldn't have to wait until historians could draw on, say, one hundred samples — which would put the date of the first legitimate nomothetic study of history somewhere between the years 30,000 and 50,000 A.D. Our knowledge of human affairs spans a mere two hundred generations, and that's a very short time.

TOYNBEE Charles G. Darwin, of my generation, wrote a book called *The Next Million Years,* a sort of *tour de force,* in which he says ten is a very large number. He was a mathematical physicist, and he knew what he was talking about. He meant that with a specimen of ten, one has a sufficient number for dealing with human affairs. Whether he was right or wrong, I was impressed by this because I had twenty or thirty, whereas he thought he could operate with ten. I'm not a mathematician — he is; he comprehends the laws of probability — I don't.

But disregarding this for the moment — could we draw statistically valid generalizations about human behavior if we had, say, 30,000 years of recorded history at our disposal? Well, I think we might analyze the operation of political constitutions in the same way as statisticians analyze all relevant facts when a person takes out fire insurance or burglary insurance. Aristotle was in fact doing this kind of thing in his *Politics* when he compared Greek local constitutions, for he realized that the greater the number the more one could generalize with accuracy. My guess is that we could bring a great deal more history within the nomothetic range than we can now, but probably not all of it. Apart from whether free will is genuine or illusory, the facts that we have the sensation of being free to choose, that we make decisions, are matters of experience, and this makes for a built-in unpredictability in human affairs. However much the increased length and elaborate documentation of history might help us to reduce this element of unpredictability, there would always be an irreducible remnant left, and this remnant is usually the most important element in the study of history. This is my *guess* — it may express a prejudice, but if so, I am arguing, so to speak, against myself now.

Coming to the question of a nomothetic versus a purely idiographic type of history, it was Lord Samuel (a friend of mine although I was a much younger man) who said to me that he thought I was making a shot — not at a study of history, but at a comprehensive study of human affairs. I think he was right, because conventional history is human affairs seen in the time dimension of human affairs. If the only human being had been Adam, if there had been no Eve and no descendants, the biography of Adam would be a single-track movement through time. But as man is a mammal, he could not produce progeny without there being at least one male and one female. Thus human society has to be at least dual, and it has actually been plural, there being simultaneously in existence in the world hundreds of millions of human beings, hundreds of thousands of human communities, perhaps at the same moment five or six civilizations, several higher religions, and so on, all moving in the time dimension side by side. Because there is this contemporaneity of events, you cannot deal with human affairs purely in terms of the time dimension — you can deal with these large numbers of parallel time movements only comparatively. It is only because we have fallen into the error of chopping up the study of human affairs into history, anthropology, psychology, sociology, etc., that history has become synonymous with an idiographic view. If you look at human history as a whole, you can see that from one aspect it may be idiographic, but when you see it in the round it is nomothetic as well; you can't escape this multiplicity of contemporaneous persons, institutions, and events — you *can* only deal with these by comparison, and comparison involves questions of likenesses and differences. The moment you get into that, you are getting into the student of non-human nature's nomothetic approach to reality.

Anthropologists, sociologists, and psychologists are all trying to find nomothetic regularities, and for some reason this is thought to be legitimate, but it is considered to be less legitimate, or not legitimate at all, when historians try it. I don't know why that is — these are all approaches to facets of human life, they are parts of the common study of human affairs. Nevertheless, the psychologists and sociologists get away with it, but the historians don't. I don't know whether the ordinary man feels the same skepticism about sociology as he does about the nomothetic approach to history.

URBAN   I think he doesn't because he feels that the facts of sociology are all in the present and very numerous: One can collect and measure them and represent them in graphs more easily than the historian's information which — as you said earlier in this talk — is complex, elusive, and subjective.

Supposing this were the true explanation, wouldn't that mean that future historians of our oppressively documented age — starting somewhere around the beginning of the century — could deal with their material with the same assurance as sociologists do with theirs? Their problem wouldn't be any scantiness of information or the arbitrary survival or destruction of past evidence, but rather an *embarras de richesse*. Wouldn't that restrict the historian's freedom to re-enact history in his own mental image and make history more reliable and respectable?

Of course, if I think of the history of the First World War or of the Yugoslav, Hungarian, and Czechoslovak upheavals in the postwar period, I am struck by the fact that all the elaborate information we possess about these events has not eliminated, or even lightened, the historian's burden. But then I am tempted to ascribe this failure to our proximity to these events and to our inevitable involvement.

TOYNBEE   My wife and I spent a large part of our working lives writing an annual *Survey of International Affairs* (for the Royal Institute of International Affairs) for which we did not have access to official documents. Now, in studying Greek and Roman history one is very conscious of the fragmentariness of what survives, and it's perfectly true that the man in the street

21

might be very skeptical about the work of a student of Greek and Roman history because so much of it is guesswork and reconstruction from conjecture. I have had the curious experience of having written, in the '20s and '30s, about events on which the documents have since been published. Certainly when the inside material becomes available — the German documents after the end of the Second World War and the British archives under the thirty-year rule — things look very different. But do you ever get the full story?

I'm very conscious of historians who think that documents from the files of government departments are like geological strata — that they are objective evidence. If you've worked in a government department, taking part in the making of documents, you become very skeptical — not that people are deliberately trying to conceal the facts to confuse the historian, but all documents are written for practical purposes, in a hurry and under pressure, and what is common knowledge in "official circles" is taken for granted. You don't waste words in minutes or a memorandum for the information of the historian, telling things that everyone concerned in the action at the moment is aware of. So, often the documents don't mention the key points, and unless you have the knowledge not given you by the documents, you may be very much misled by the documents. I'm conscious of this, having been on the inside as well as on the outside. Therefore, I'm not sure that having a complete documentation of human affairs would change the nature of the historian's work. I'm sure that we shall have, over the next century, very much more extensive documentation than we have of Byzantine or Greek or Roman history, but I'm not sure that this will make history more credible. It's still going to be the question not only of subjective selection from this enormous mass of information, but of the information that isn't given, because it has been taken for granted by the people who were recording the information. I don't know how we'll get over this problem — it might apply not only to history but to sociology and anthropology, though not perhaps to psychology, which is trying to burrow underneath the information.

URBAN You don't think documents are manufactured — or destroyed — to mislead the historian and to justify politicians and policies? One is familiar enough with the literature of self-justification *post factum*, but is there any conscious anticipation of history at the time of action?

TOYNBEE After the Second World War some of the first important books to come out were a spate of memoirs, including very carefully selected documents, by French politicians who had played a poor part in the war. They wanted to get in first and justify themselves. But I don't know whether, for instance, Churchill (who was in his own right a very distinguished historian) had a second eye on history when he wrote a memorandum or minutes or when he made a speech during the war. It is true that — against all security rules — he kept carbon copies of his documents and took them away with him, but on the whole, this kind of practice is rare. Government business is so enormous, civil servants and ministers are so hard pressed, running from pillar to post, that they haven't time for luxuries like posthumous self-justification. Churchill himself was very strict on this: He would make extensive use of the telephone, write in longhand and write very short reports, as the situation demanded. There was no room for self-justification.

URBAN How did your *Survey of International Affairs* of the '20s and '30s actually stand up to scrutiny when the official documents became available?

TOYNBEE Restricting myself to the time from Hitler's rise to power to the outbreak of war — my wife and I found that information was harder and harder to get because governments were all becoming much more cagey about their activities. What we did in our *Survey* was to give alternative possible explanations of the facts as we knew them and of the purposes we suspected behind them. When we got the published German documents — at that stage we did not get the British sources — we found that none of our alternatives was entirely correct, but I don't think we were ever completely wrong.

URBAN Could one hope to deal sensibly with the explosion of historical information by putting it through the computer? Is there some formula whereby computers could be so programmed as to distill from the historical material laws, or at least regularities, with predictive value for our future?

TOYNBEE If I'm right in thinking that there are certain built-in uniformities in human nature, computerization should bring out some of them. Take my old friend Sir Lewis Namier — supposing his great collection of biographies of eighteenth century British Members of Parliament were computerized (unfortunately for himself, Namier just missed the computer age), I dare say these biographies could be so processed through computers that the individual actions and careers of these M.P.s could be expressed in terms of certain underlying permanent and uniform facts of human nature. Or take the case of a General Election. We know the results in terms of quantification — the majority and minority for this party or that, but we don't know the relation between the individual voter's fluctuations of feelings during the election period and the final outcome of the vote. Computerization could deal with the large masses of data involved; it could probably produce a rational relation between the way the voters were feeling and thinking and the final election figures. At present, since we have not computerized the information, we can't do this. Therefore, I think computers might make a great difference in shaping history into a more precise form of study and knowledge.

URBAN Would they put historians out of business in the sense of eliminating the process of weighing and selecting?

TOYNBEE No, I can't see how they could do that. The person who programs the computer and the person who receives and interprets the results of computerization is still an individual at a point of space-time, with his own subjective attitude toward human affairs — a computer can't become a human soul so to speak, and, if it did, it would have its own bias.

URBAN I feel the criterion of objectivity is still eluding us. If the historian is a child of his time and if his activity as a "maker" of facts gives him an unconscious bias, isn't there nevertheless a minimum body of facts and rules which he must observe or else incur the odium of his fellow historians, even though he may get away with hoodwinking the public? One could wish that history — like physical nature — had some way of offering a "fact barrier" to those trying to force their way through it at excessive speeds or at tortuous angles.

Mightn't there be a clue to this problem in modern physics which tells us that we can determine either the speed *or* the mass of a moving particle, but not both? Couldn't one say that the historian who discerns patterns and laws in history writes "speed history," hence he is perhaps weak on detail, while the one who is content to assemble and analyze the bones of history writes "mass history," hence he is more likely to be poor in vision?

TOYNBEE We can't help having unconscious axes to grind to some extent, but there is a difference between the unconscious and the conscious and deliberate manipulation of historical information, though, as I have said, the unconscious is intrinsically harder to correct. If you have a nomothetic way of dealing with human affairs you must believe there is something permanent and regular in history, just as the physicist or chemist believes there is something regular in material nature. The permanent and regular element in human affairs is human nature — the whole psychosomatic unity of a human being. If you believe that the nomothetic approach is possible in human affairs, then I would say the objective criterion is this uniformity and constancy of human nature, though, because of the trickiness, elusiveness, and complexity of human affairs, obviously an historian cannot be so successful as the physicist can. As far as we know, human nature has not varied since the earliest date at which our ancestors became recognizably human, which is a recent date, of course, compared to the age of the physical universe. No doubt human nature, like everything in the universe, is changing all the time, but the change since our ancestors first became human has been so minute that for practical purposes we can regard human nature from the beginning till the present time, and for the foreseeable future, as constant. That is the basis for a possible nomothetic study, and it is my contention — which I believe is important and right — that we must study human affairs as a whole and not as a chaotic heap of spillikins. The study of human affairs goes awry when it is broken up into a number of "disciplines" insulated from each other by water-tight compartments: history, poetry, religion, psychology, anthropology, sociology, etc. That said, the work of the historian who cultivates only a small patch of land is of very great importance not only as a piece of idiographic activity but for the nomothetic historian too who has to build on his findings. Ideally, therefore, history is the result of the work (if you like) of both "speed historians" and "mass historians," although it is very seldom that the two approaches are successfully pursued by the same man.

URBAN You are challenging academic demarcation lines, specialization, the Ph.D. industry, and many other sacred cows of our time. Your critics, in turn, have not been slow to challenge you as a man with an axe to grind. Have these attacks led you to change your mind about the validity of your method as a nomothetic historian?

TOYNBEE They have led me to think that in some cases I pushed my nomothetic scheme too far. It has been proved against me that this or that regularity, recurrence, or law which I thought I saw, was an illusion. But all this has not cured me of thinking that not only is it possible but that it is necessary, in studying human affairs, to have a nomothetic approach as well as an idiographic approach.

One of my strongest critics was Pitirim Sorokin, the Russian sociologist at Harvard. I admire him for his adventurousness. As you know, his work consists of trying to apply the statistical approach (quantification is the word nowadays) to all sides of human life. Now, you can obviously apply this nomothetic method to things like the insurance business, or to catering, but he has applied it to art, philosophy, religion, and psychology — he has been trying to see how far you can go in quantification. He has obviously gone too far, but I think he has done a service by showing by experiment the limits of quantification in human affairs. He was a rather naïve man, believing that he was absolutely right and his critics were all wrong. I am more tentative — I am more ready to listen to my critics than he was, which I think is not a weakness but a strength.

Coming back to myself, I would say that in very many particulars I profited from my critics and thought again, but on the question of the nomothetic approach I am unrepentant. I would say that the people who learn more and more about less and less by rejecting everything they can't quantify in history are themselves applying the nomothetic approach to history, but applying it very poorly. Some of my bitterest critics have gone recklessly into quantification, far beyond what I should think was wise or possible. The borderline between what is and what isn't history has always been elusive. For instance, an historical novel isn't history, and an historian is acutely conscious of the difference. He may like an historical novel, but he has a certain shrinking from it because it is deliberately tampering with the phenomena which the historian works on, and for that reason the historical novelist is an artist more than he is an historian. In that sense the historian is not an artist — he is not like a novelist or a poet. But there is another sense which I touched on at the end of my *Study* — a sense of awe and wonder at human destiny, and human affairs in general, in which the historian is on common ground with the poet or the visual artist. So perhaps he is half-way between the scientist and the poet. There is a kind of snobbery in calling history a science. It is not and cannot be a science in the sense in which physics or chemistry is a science.

URBAN I suspect the snobbery increases as the respectability of one's discipline decreases. I sometimes wonder whether this snobbery isn't simply a compensation for a sense of inferiority — whether one couldn't lay it down as a rule that the weaker your social "science," the heavier the jargon it employs, i.e., the stronger the need for camouflage. There is something pathetic about a discipline which is not only incapable of evolving a method *sui generis,* but also prides itself on living in the reflected methodological glory of another.

TOYNBEE The historians in the fashion are very much on the defensive. This is ironical, for they are both in the fashion and they feel that they are the orthodox — people like me are heretics. At the same time they are very unsure of their position — they aren't sure whether they may not be overturned. Sometimes they have an almost personal animus against me. I have always been curious as to why this is — it's like the personal animus against an anarchist or a communist: This man may subvert our whole way of life, or thought, or work; he is a dangerous beast, we must put him down. That is a sign, I think, of defensiveness and weakness. This hostility to me, and the aping of the scientists, are really incompatible with each other but, as I say, the same men hold both attitudes.

URBAN Historians have become extremely censorious of each other, and I would say the British historians are second to none in the acrimony with which they try to discredit each other's reputations —

TOYNBEE — it's the *odium theologicum* of our time. There is a difference between British and non-British historians, but there is also — as I know from the reviews of different installments of my book — a difference between pre-Second World War historians and post-Second World War historians on this point of acrimony, temper, and animus. The first six volumes of my *Study* were reviewed before the Second World War; some of the reviews were just as critical, just as condemnatory, if you like, as later reviews, but they were all good tempered and polite, and however strongly they censured me, there was no kind of personal, or even abstract, hostility. Since the war it's not only I who've been savagely attacked by his fellow historians, and I'm not sure that the viciousness of the infighting is peculiar to historians. If you took a sample of British reviews of poetry, novels, and scientific works you would probably find the same. I've thought about this a good deal, and I suspect the acrimony has something to do with the unhappy things that have happened to the British since the war. It may be a consciousness of Britain having become a second-class power instead of a first-class power. We have, by the standards of past empires, behaved rather well — we left India before we were kicked out, and have decolonized our whole empire; we have accepted the fact that the pound is not the world's reserve currency, and that we are a minor nuclear power. But while on the surface a nation may seem reasonable, underneath it she may be subconsciously boiling, and this comes out in bitterness and aggressiveness. There are cases in history in which a big reverse in a country's relations with the outer world is followed by fratricidal wars. Take fifteenth century English history: We had one of our biggest reverses in Joan of Arc; we were pushed out of France ignominiously, but immediately after, instead of feeling that they were companions in misfortune, the English fought a very brutal civil war, the Wars of the Roses. So this infighting and the savagery may be the psychological effects of having come down in the world and having to try to digest the reverses. Does this sound like a reasonable explanation?

URBAN I think it does. I would add only one point: The malevolence of British historians has a comfortable lead over the suspicions and jealousies of poets, novelists, and scientists. When a British historian is unhappy with the work of another, he is seldom content to play the ball — he will play the player. He will not only question the other man's findings or method, but he will cast doubt on his competence, he will try to discredit his personal integrity — he is after his blood. There is perhaps an ideological element in this asperity, as history is nearer the bone than science or fiction.

TOYNBEE British historians of the postwar generation have a very strongly held view that they ought to be "professional," that they ought to write for other professional specialists and not for the general public. At the same time they are conscious that this emphasis on professionalism is alienating them from the public whom they affect to despise but whom they cannot afford to lose; and they subconsciously recognize that if they only write for each other, they will cease to count. But when did the term "professional historian" first gain currency? Probably when history writing became the preserve of the universities, because until fairly recently the most eminent British historians were what would now be called amateurs. I've seen Veronica Wedgewood criticized as an amateur because she has never been a university teacher. This is absurd.

URBAN G. R. Elton lists Acton among the amateurs and he says the work of both Gibbon and Macaulay is overshadowed by the lesser but more professional historians of our time.

TOYNBEE Obviously Professor Elton is an extremely able man, and anyone would agree with a great deal of what he says in *The Practice of History,* but certain things stand out in my mind — especially the number of times he uses the words "professional" and, to a certain extent, "trained" and "lay." He is almost obsessive about them. Clearly, Elton regards himself as "professional" and "trained," whereas he regards Gibbon, Acton, Macaulay, and G. M. Trevelyan as being "lay." He doesn't anywhere positively define what he means by the difference between "professional" and "lay," but he implies in the section on the teaching of history that "professional" is somebody who has taken a Ph.D. degree under the supervision of an instructor who himself has taken a Ph.D. degree under the supervision of an instructor, and the pupil will, in turn, instruct other people who are taking Ph.D. degrees. When this categorization "professional/nonprofessional" had not yet been invented, it was much harder to accuse someone of not being an historian. Today there is a very simple test: Are you a member of a university faculty (preferably with a Ph.D. degree), or are you not? If you are, you are an historian. If you are not, you're for it. Gibbon, Acton, Macaulay, were all "lay" historians. They would have been horrified to be called professionals, for they would have thought this was implying that they cut themselves off from the general, cultivated public and had, in a sense, barbarized themselves. They thought of themselves primarily as just cultivated human beings in discourse with other cultivated human beings. Elton is trying deliberately to create a closed circuit of "professional" historians which is, in my opinion, fatal to any form of study. At the back of his mind Elton is probably conscious of this weakness, and perhaps this explains the mixture of arrogance and defensiveness of his book.

URBAN Not surprisingly, Elton is very critical of your own approach to history. He says in one place that the term historian does not include "the great system-makers, such as A. J. Toynbee . . . selection of evidence on that scale, to prove a foreordained case, removes the practitioner from the ranks of historians. Of course, his proper title may be more honorific: some people like prophets, especially of doom."

TOYNBEE I thought this was a glorious free advertisement. When I went up to Oxford as an undergraduate to study Greek and Latin, my tutor gave me some preliminary advice. He said: "I should advise you, as you're a beginner, not to read Professor Gilbert Murray's books and not to go to his lectures, because he is a very dangerous man." Well, I immediately rushed to the college library and got out as many of Gilbert Murray's books as I could, and went to his lectures and discovered, of course, that he was much more illuminating than my poor tutor was. Now, with that in mind, if I were today an undergraduate, and read those remarks of Professor Elton, I should rush to read my own works, and if I read a book of some anti-Elton saying the same sort of things about Elton, I would make it my business to read Professor Elton's books.

URBAN Professor Elton's case against you is mainly methodological, but I believe some of your critics' personal animus has more to do with your philosophy than your professionalism and method, although those who object to one often object to the other two as well. It has to do with your faith, with the apocalyptic view you take of human destiny and the religious imagery in which you sometimes express yourself. These things are supposed to be presumptuous and humorless. In any case, they are unfashionable — that plus your success should explain the animus.

Hugh Trevor-Roper, for instance, in a very bitter and extremely personal attack against you in *Encounter*, said in so many words that he found the character of your work not only erroneous but "hateful":

> Toynbee does not only utter false arguments and dogmatic statements, calling them "scientific" and "empirical"; he does not only preach a gospel of deliberate obscurantism; he seems to undermine our will, welcome our defeat, gloat over the extinction of our civilization, not because he supports the form of civilization which threatens us, but because he is animated by what we can only call a masochistic desire to be conquered. If Hitler and Stalin rejoiced in the prospect of destroying the West, theirs at least was a crude, intelligible rejoicing. They smacked their lips because they looked for plunder. Toynbee has no such interests in supporting a conqueror. He hungers spiritually for our defeat.

TOYNBEE   I made some personal enquiries because I was concerned and curious about Trevor-Roper's attack. Apparently he thinks I have deliberately set out to be a prophet and to lay the foundations of a future cult. This is of course quite fantastic, but the fact that he, I'm sure bona fide, believes this to be true throws light on his own thinking. I was told he has an almost physical horror of my attitude to life. Now in our talk today we have already seen the real justification of Trevor-Roper's view that I am prophetic, in the sense that I care immensely about what is going to happen after I am dead. As to Trevor-Roper's imputation that I somehow relished the prospect of the Western democracies' collapse under the impact of nazism, I can only say that this is nonsense, and it is not even plausible nonsense. All through the Second World War I was working day and night for the British Government, and my reactions were like those of the rest of the British: In 1940 I didn't see how we could possibly win, but I assumed, like everybody else here, that we would go on fighting. And when the news came of Pearl Harbor, I thought to myself, why, Hitler has lost the war — I was thrilled and exhilarated at the prospect that we were going to be on the winning side after all. No, Trevor-Roper labors under an illusion. If you were to ask people at the Foreign Office for whom I was working during the war, they might say I was doing my job efficiently or inefficiently, but they would certainly say I was working whole heartedly for the victory of Britain and the defeat of Hitler. I thought it would be the most terrible thing for Europe if Hitler won. One must distinguish between not seeing how Hitler could fail to win, which was very difficult to see in 1940, and wishing Hitler to win. I never wished Hitler to win — with all my heart I wished him to lose and be defeated.

URBAN Trevor-Roper, to do him justice, didn't say in so many words that you were hoping or working for nazi victory — although he did say that you were the unconscious intellectual ally of Hitler in the non-nazi world; the brunt of his attack was that the Second World War did not bring about the death of our civilization — which it ought to have done if there was truth in the laws of your *Study* — and that you were consequently disappointed. The years 1939-45 did not, he says, change your eagerness to see the West destroyed.

TOYNBEE I'm a Westerner, I have a stake in the West's future, I value Western civilization, and I don't want to see it go under. Secondly, I have always been a great anti-imperialist, a supporter of the underdog. I have always wanted to see the domination of the West over the rest of the world reduced again to its normal position of equality with the other present-day civilizations. For instance, I was thoroughly in favor of the British Labor Government giving independence to India, Pakistan, and Ceylon in 1947, but this is different from wishing the West to disappear. I have often written that the West is a minority in numbers, and, as technological superiority is a wasting asset because in time other people learn what the West has invented, it is very important — and in the West's interest — that we should come down to a footing of equality in good time, rather than be overthrown, clinging to power, and then have the roles reversed. But this is not anti-Western — it is pro-Western: a wish for the preservation of the Western civilization as one among a number of different civilizations.

The West's ascendancy over the rest of the world during the last three centuries has been reflected in the recent Western way of looking at mankind's history as all leading up to the modern West. I think this West-centered view of history is a palpable case of subjectivism; it seems to me to misrepresent the reality and, in so far as it distorts it, to make it unintelligible.

In the third place, I have always been very cautious in prophesying about living civilizations because I realize that I'm in the middle of the story. I have always said that retrospectively I can see the patterns, the regularities of history — though I recognize that this is very controversial — but that one cannot spot current or future patterns and prophesy that the West is or is not going to fall, or that any other thing is or is not going to happen. It is impossible to do this because there is — or so it seems to me — an element of unpredictability, of free will in human affairs. For all these reasons Trevor-Roper's attack on me on this point is not borne out by what I've said or done.

I would say Trevor-Roper himself is not entirely detached — no human being can be. We are all actors in the drama we are watching. Perhaps in studying atoms and electrons, a human being can be purely a spectator (I'm not even sure about that), but certainly in studying other human beings' behavior he cannot be purely a spectator; he can be a spectator but he is also a participant, even if the other human being is paleolithic man, because we are all part of human society, we all share in human destiny — we are involved. I think it is an illusion to imagine that the historian can escape from this personal involvement: If you could escape from it you would really stultify yourself for dealing with human affairs, because in saying that now I have to discard one kind of enquiry because it would be subjective, and then another because it would be political or prophetic, by the time you had finished you'd have discarded the study of human affairs and said: I've got to be a physicist or mathematician, I cannot study human affairs at all. This comes out in quantification. The possibility of quantifying some aspect of human activity successfully varies in inverse ratio to the human importance of that particular aspect. This comes out very clearly in those fascinating tables in Sorokin's books: He is most successful where his tables matter least.

URBAN   I feel some of Trevor-Roper's imputations are too farfetched to be taken at face value. Nevertheless, your conception of the role of history and of the historian is so elevated that one could call it religious without, I believe, violating your meaning. Your *Study* is certainly a theodicy: "History," you tell us, is "a vision . . . of God revealing Himself in action to souls that were sincerely seeking Him." Indeed, in the words of one of your critics, Crane Brinton, your *Study* is "a 'City of God' . . . in which evidence taken from the historical record . . . is used to transcend history." You are deeply conscious of the sinfulness of man, the fragility of human institutions, the idolization of man by man, and the blasphemy of state worship. I have to make a fairly crude distinction here: Are we to think of you as a historian who is being — perhaps reluctantly — propelled toward sainthood by the momentum of his work, or is your religious apparatus a device for telling your story and driving home your message in the highest spiritual form, i.e., depicting man's march through time in the language and symbolism of that creative minority whose social milieu — as you say — "spoke to them . . . of History" rather than of the pressing problems of everyday life?

There is certainly no shortage of evidence to support the first proposition. Let me quote two passages from your *Study*. The first shows your trust in the mystic unity of history, poetry, and religion; in the second you say that the historian's experience brings him to "the threshold of the saint's communion with God." In volume X of your *Study* you say:

It is no wonder that . . . the historians should have had to let the poets be their spokesmen; for the joy awakened by the dawn of a new era of History is the Soul's response to an epiphany that is something more than a merely temporal event. The dawns that awaken such joy as this are irruptions into Time out of Eternity. What has happened on these historic occasions likewise happens at the birth of every child. . . . In a mother's joy the Soul hails an incarnation; . . . the dawns of mundane eras that have this poetry in them are antitypes of cosmic dawns in which a Divine Light breaks into This World.

And later in the same volume you say:

When the feeling for the poetry in the facts of History is . . . transmuted into awe at the epiphany of God in History, the historian's inspiration is preparing him for an experience that has been described as "the Beatific Vision" by souls to whom it has been vouchsafed. In this experience, God is seen face to face, and no longer through a glass darkly; and this means that the vision carries the Soul beyond the limits of History or of any other avenue of approach towards God through His revelation of His nature in His works.

TOYNBEE The question is my personal position in time and space, of which my education is part. I have already mentioned one element in my education: Greek and Latin language and literature, Greek and Roman history, and the study of all the civilizations spreading from Greece and Rome. Another fact in my education was that I was brought up as an orthodox Anglican Christian, and I was soaked in the Bible, as well as in the Greek and Latin classics, at an impressionable age. The Bible, including biblical language, of course, and the biblical view of history, stayed with me throughout my life. Here was another form of universalism — the Jewish view, shared by Christianity and Islam, that history is the working out of a divine plan from creation to the last things. I'm not a believer. When I was an undergraduate I ceased to believe in the doctrines of Christianity; I couldn't pass muster in Christian creeds, but the Jewish-Christian-Muslim attitude toward human history obviously soaked into me and has stayed with me. This is much more universalistic than Polybius's or Herodotus's view of human affairs because it puts history into the framework of theology and metaphysics and inculcates a view of the ultimate nature of reality. None of this was deliberate or contrived — it was part of my education in the widest sense of the world — it was part of the general cultural atmosphere in which I grew up in a middle-class family in England at the turn of the century.

I'm very conscious of the tragedy of human events, of the wages of overweening pride — hybris — which accounts for so much both of the Hebrew prophets' and the Greeks' attitude to life. The Jewish and Greek attitudes are, of course, very different, but they are alike in seeing the vanity of human wishes, the nothingness of power, and the ultimate collapse of all things made by man. Studying Greek and Roman history is an eye opener to the self-destruction of the most awe-inspiring achievements of human societies.

The First World War, in which about half of my school fellows and contemporaries at the university were killed, was another formative influence. The tragedy, the senseless wickedness and futility of human life — and then I was spared because I was ill at the time and couldn't serve in the army — had an enduring effect on me. I went to two peace conferences in Paris — in 1919 and 1946 — and each time I saw things go wildly wrong and the world fall back into turmoil and chaos again. This kind of thing gives one a religious attitude toward human affairs; it makes one believe with St. Francis of Assisi that material success of any kind is vanity, delusion, and a betrayal of human nature.

URBAN   You seem to have come a long way from curiosity about history to propounding a prophetic view of it. Would I be wrong in saying that your curiosity was mixed, from the beginning, with a search for a commanding view — perhaps even an uplifting vision — of the kind Goethe had in mind when he spoke of *Enthusiasmus* in history?

TOYNBEE   I devoted my working life to history for its own sake because I had curiosity about it. I was interested in it, and I couldn't help doing it. This, I think, is a sufficient reason for studying history. However, people often tell me that this is a frivolous reason. I don't think it *is* frivolous: One of the glories of human nature is that we have curiosity about things that are not of immediate utility. Man had curiosity about the stars long before it was conceivable to him that knowledge of the stars could be of any practical use to the farmer or the navigator. If he hadn't had this distinterested curiosity, this distinctly human, supra-animal attitude to the universe, utility wouldn't have followed.

39

Now, there are different objects of curiosity. The first is phenomena — we live in the phenomena, and we have to deal with these in the first instance. But our curiosity leads us not merely to revel in the phenomena but to penetrate behind them. Scientists are trying to delve under the phenomena to the realities and to express these realities in terms of regularities and laws. The study of human affairs follows the same principle: When I study history I try to penetrate beyond the human phenomena to what lies behind them. I use the word God in trying to name what I suspect lies behind the phenomena, because I can't find any other expression. If I were talking to a Buddhist I might use the words "ultimate spiritual reality" in or behind the universe — this is what I mean. But curiosity about the phenomena isn't enough: My curiosity leads me on to be curious about the nature and meaning of destiny (if there is such a thing), about existence as a whole. In other words, for me history is a way of entering into and trying to comprehend the universe. Every human being has a feeling that life is mysterious, and every human being is to some extent trying to comprehend the incomprehensible.

URBAN It is possible to think of regularities and laws in human affairs which would not invite the historian to look at ultimate reality. There are many lowly problems which require study and which are, I believe, just as amenable to the nomothetic approach as the study of civilizations. Yet they do not lead the historian to metahistory. I suppose you would question whether these phenomena are worthy of the historian's attention.

TOYNBEE No, I think it would be illuminating, for instance, to cull information from the gossip columns, the financial and sports pages of newspapers and to find regularities in them. The laws which we would discover at these — subjectively speaking — lower levels of enterprise would tell us something about human life just as much as the nomothetic study of the "higher" levels does. After all, human life is partly lofty but partly extremely undignified and humiliatingly so. We are a painful mixture of gods and animals.

URBAN Nevertheless you feel that to conceive of history as the revelation of God in His epiphany is not only a loftier but also a truer (that is, a more realistic) way of approaching reality than dwelling on the workaday aspects of human affairs.

TOYNBEE I do feel that. It may have been the Bible in my infancy that makes me feel that, but the Greek historians too — although they were not theodicists, although they didn't think in the framework of an omnipotent God like the Jews and Christians — had this notion of mysterious power in the background. Fortune was almost personified as a goddess by Polybius, and Herodotus is full of the envy of the gods and the humbling of human pride. The Greeks (and the Chinese for that matter) are more pedestrian about this than the Hebrew prophets, but man's awe in the presence of an inscrutable divine power is unmistakably there.

URBAN Do you feel this power is relevant to us today even though our lives have been emptied of God and the symbolism of religion?

TOYNBEE Yes, I do. I'll put it negatively: Man is a spiritual being besides being a psychosomatic organism and part of the material universe. But it's ludicrous to suppose that he's the highest form of spiritual life in existence or conceivable. He is so imperfect and is such a tragic mixture of the lofty and the obscene that it is absurd to think of him as being the highest thing in creation. This is, of course, an act of faith — I can't demonstrate it. It's a negative conclusion from my judgment of human nature.

*   *   *

URBAN On the fourth page of the first volume of your *Study*, published in 1934, you come out strongly against specialization and the industrialization of the study of history.

Since the days of Mommsen and Ranke, historians have given their best energies to the "assemblage" of raw materials . . . and, when they have attempted to "work" these materials "up" into "manufactured" or "semi-manufactured" articles, they have had recourse . . . to the Division of Labour and have produced synthetic histories like the several series of volumes now in course of publication by the Cambridge University Press. Such series are monuments to the laboriousness, the "factual" knowledge, the mechanical skill, and the organizing power of our society. They will take their rank with our stupendous tunnels and bridges and dams and liners and battleships and skyscrapers, and their editors will be remembered among the famous Western engineers. In invading the realm of historical thought, the Industrial System has given scope to great strategists and has set up marvellous trophies of victory. Yet, in a detached onlooker's mind, the doubt arises whether this conquest may not, after all, be a *tour de force* and the confidence of victory the delusion of a false analogy.

Since these words were written historians have tunneled much deeper on shrinking plots, and the study of history as a whole has become even more like a factory cooperative, with models and methods drawn from a variety of sciences — both "hard" and "social." Your own work is, of course, a plea against this kind of history. Can you see the tunnelers come out of their rabbit warrens and take a larger and — for the reader — less tedious view of human affairs?

TOYNBEE The extreme technologization of history has a very unfortunate, paralyzing effect on historians: Any historian who tries to re-enlarge his field is terrified of being caught out by someone who cultivates a more minute field and who has, therefore, a more microscopic view of the facts. He will be told he's wrong on this and wrong on that — he'll be confuted and paralyzed. One unfortunate effect of this is that the public

42

tends to ignore the specialists. These men, the public think, are writing for each other, not for us — we needn't pay any attention to them. It is at this stage that the popularizers jump in who are rightly criticized by the so-called professional historians for writing with inadequate knowledge and writing just to please. What we want is first class minds to address an intelligent but nonspecialized public. The French are very good at this. Their "vulgarizations," as they call them ironically, are very often the best and most highly prized works of French *savants*. But I'm not sure whether we are going to get this any longer. It seems as if the French were going the same way as the Germans, the Americans, and the British.

URBAN Is your great popularity, especially in America since the Second World War, to be explained in terms of a reaction to the atomization of knowledge and the isolation and moral nonalignment of specialized historians? Or are we simply witnessing a periodic change in tastes? Your popularity in America astounds me, for your *Study* is very exacting reading; it demands a grounding in the classics which is not one of the qualities American education favors. Yet your *Study* is not only read but definitely fashionable. The same goes, to a lesser degree, for Germany, where the classical background is, of course, much more firmly established.

TOYNBEE I've asked a number of Americans about this because suddenly, just after the end of the Second World War, Summervell's abridgment of my first six volumes became practically a best seller in America, and consequently the full version of the book began to sell too. Americans told me that the American people as a whole became very conscious that this was a turning point in their history. They had been isolationists since the beginning of American history, they had tried to build up an earthly paradise in the New World and jump clear of the evils of the old. Now they had been implicated — twice over — in great wars, and they realized that they couldn't get out of the world after all. This was a terrible shock, and they were casting about for new orientations: What is America's place in the world; what is mankind's place in the universe? Their whole picture was suddenly shattered by their involvement in two world wars. My book came along at this moment: "Perhaps," they thought, "this man is going to give us a chart which will enable us to take our bearings," as if Columbus had been lost in the middle of the Atlantic and a chart had drifted his way to show him some landfalls.

The German case is rather different. Germans have always managed to pursue both sides of historiography at once: They have been tremendous detailed researchers, and they have also had large views. It is true that Mommsen became slightly apologetic after a time about his brilliant *Roman History* — with hindsight he thought it was amateurish. But in the next generation German historiography had people like Eduard Meyer who could comprehend the whole of ancient history from the original sources — pretty well the last man who was able to do so. So the Germans always had this eagerness to generalize, to see the whole, to philosophize about history, and that, I think, gave me an entry into Germany.

A word about changing fashion. If one reads Gibbon, one is struck by his very generous acknowledgments of his debts to the seventeenth century men of learning — he is very frank about his debt to those great compilations of material which the seventeenth century left behind. He's consciously like Solomon to David: His seventeenth century predecessors collected the materials for the temple and that enabled him to build the temple. The seventeenth century scholars were rather like the twentieth century historians — they were interested in minute details, collecting inscriptions, documents, charters, and so on. But in the eighteenth century there was a change of fashion: The eighteenth century scholars were impatient — they didn't want to be collectors, sorters, and annotators. They were very glad to use what the seventeenth century scholars had done for them, and Gibbon, whenever he comes to the end of some great compilation and can't rely on it any more, notes this and bewails the fact that he is now rather at sea compared to the previous period. This points to an important change in outlook — perhaps change of fashion is too slighting a way to put it: It's pointless to have collected a great deal of information unless it is used; and when you've used it for building up comprehensive pictures, like Polybius's or Gibbon's, you find that you have run beyond your information, and the next generation will probably feel the importance of getting more information. So there is perhaps an alternating rhythm in the style of historical scholarship —

URBAN — both history and historiography moving in cycles —

TOYNBEE — yes, and it would be healthy if people realized and recognized that both activities are necessary and particularly that both are necessary to each other. The present fight between the generalist and the specialist is ludicrous because neither of them could do his job without the other.

URBAN Sticking to one's little patch of land also has another advantage: It relieves the historian of any necessity to ask questions about the legitimacy and morality of human actions. Judgments are suspended and moral issues avoided. I think this is a great evil. One of the virtues of your book is that it does take sides. You do stick your neck out.

TOYNBEE I came across this problem in different contexts. When my wife and I wrote our *Survey of International Affairs,* our instructions were to be scientific, which meant objective — to write as if we weren't directly concerned. Now this was all right in writing an account of the dispute between the Netherlands and Belgium about their respective rights in the waters of the river Scheldt. But when it came to Hitler's seizure of power and the Italian invasion of Ethiopia — how can one, in the scientific sense, be impartial and objective about that? *Could* one be objective? A. J. P. Taylor's book on nazi Germany — purposely provocative perhaps — shows Hitler as an ordinary politician pursuing a *Realpolitik* like any other, so why brand him specially? One can do this if one suspends judgment. The distinction between right and wrong, and the conviction that you ought to support the right and oppose the wrong, is something innate in human nature — you can't get away from it. If I had written of Hitler at his genocide stage as if I were writing a weather report (in the same jaunty way in which the B.B.C. announces the weather reports), I shouldn't have been really impartial: I should have been siding with Hitler, I should have been treating something evil as if it were normal, even good and ordinary. This is the kind of difficulty which, as you say, the historians who won't make moral judgments are shirking.

URBAN Any discussion of the history of the Soviet Union runs into the same difficulty. There is (especially in America) a certain reluctance among scholars to speak of the Soviet system as a dictatorship, although this is what the Soviets themselves call it. One doesn't talk of totalitarianism either because that, too, is supposed to imply value judgment, so that the long despotic rule of Stalin is discussed under some innocuous heading such as "industrializing society" or "command economy." The idea is, indeed, to impose the style of the B.B.C.'s weather report, and to make evil things look, as you say, normal and ordinary. There are also many other ways of doctoring the Soviet record, especially the chapter on forced industrialization, which lends itself more easily to discussion in a purely economic framework than the great terror or the deportation of nationalities.

TOYNBEE   But even on the level of describing the industrialization of Russia, one is giving a distorted picture because industrialization, like any human business, has a right and a wrong side, a spiritual side to it. One couldn't describe the industrial revolution in this country without discussing the hardships, the miseries, the injustices that accompanied it, as well as the economic, technological, and statistical facts. It would be an unreal account if you didn't take the human side into account as well. In Russia the brutalities were far more extreme. So I think eliminating the moral factor is a dead end.

*   *   *

URBAN   We have now seen (if I may draw some conclusions at this point) that writing history is a dangerous activity, because, consciously or unconsciously, it is bound to serve present positions; but we have also seen that it is almost impossible to write history in any other way. Wouldn't we then be better off *without* history? If one is a keen European, for instance, one is rather appalled at the pains we all take in our various national parishes to maintain the memory of ancient feuds and rivalries and the crimes we have committed against each other. Wouldn't the Irish people be better off if the Battle of the Boyne and all that came after had not been quite so scrupulously kept alive in their consciousness? I think the Americans, for whom history is not a very prestigious activity, may have given us a lead here. Shouldn't historians advocate the suspension of their own discipline as a first step toward peace? Of course, it would be difficult to put any such thing into practice, but, in an ideal world, wouldn't it be a step in the right direction if the world obtained a 100-year armistice from its historians and, indeed, an Orwellian ban on historical memory: no history books, no remembrance-day celebrations, no expellees' organizations, no campaign medals worn at garden parties, no streets and underground stations named after victorious massacres, no commemorations of revolutions until, say, a 100 years have elapsed and the passions are spent?

TOYNBEE An old friend of mine, Sir Alfred Zimmern, who was a don when I was an undergraduate at Oxford, pointed out to me that most people in the world have no sense of history, that the past doesn't exist for them, that people who have any consciousness of history are a small minority. This was a startling thought to me but it *is* true. Would historic amnesia help? Think of American history since the end of the Second World War: Haven't the Americans rushed into an awful lot of blunders through ignoring history almost as a matter of principle? They rushed into the war in Vietnam, deliberately ignoring French experience. They thought they had the power, the technology, and the American way of life which made the French experience irrelevant. A great many of America's failures since the Second World War can be put down to not looking at the present in the light of the past. Human life is lived in time-depth; present action takes place not merely in anticipation of the future but in the light of the past. If you deliberately ignore, think away, or deface the past, you're hampering yourself for taking intelligent action in the present.

URBAN The fashionable thing in America is not only to ignore the past but to downgrade the present too. One of America's popular "futurologists," Alvin Toffler, argues in *Future Shock* that we should study the present from the vantage point of the future: "It is no longer sufficient for Johnny to understand the past. It is not even enough for him to understand the present, for the here-and-now environment will soon vanish. He must learn to anticipate the directions and rate of change." One could match this from other American sources: They stress — and I often feel they revel in — the "temporary society," the "throw-away-civilization," the "ad-hocracy," and other concepts which denote shifting relationships and are consequently hostile to history.

TOYNBEE It would be a useful type of spiritual discipline and a humbling thought for people acting, say, on armament or pollution, to imagine what their great-grandchildren will think of their activities — about their apportionment of energy and resources, and the attention they paid to different sides of life. Then, of course, we all plan for the future: A person plans his career, he tries to save for old age, he brings up a family, he thinks of their education; statesmen think ahead in their policies, or they ought to anyway.

In the eighteenth century, for instance, people thought ahead of their distant descendants. They would build homes and plant trees and make very long-range dispositions: The future of the family or of the dynasty was a very important consideration in the material, social, and spiritual sense. Our attitude today is very different: National budgets and businesses are run on a year to year or a month to month basis which is an immature way of looking at the world. One of the evils of the industrial system is weekly wages; most people think in terms of the period they are paid in, and weekly wages mean that people think in terms of a few days only at a time. This is a great weakness.

URBAN What exactly do we lose when we lose the dimension of history? The idea that our situation is unique, that the lessons of the past have no relevance to us are pretty widespread, not only in America but in Europe too.

TOYNBEE I think we lose a sense of the realities, especially of the weaknesses and limitations, of human life. The thought that our age is unique is a form of pride which derives from a false view of the power and excellence of human life. It has hap-

49

pened before: In the Renaissance the medieval schoolmen were dismissed; at the time of Alexander's conquest the previous history of Greece was dismissed as not worth thinking about. Greek historians equated the beginning of history with the crossing of the Hellespont by Alexander the Great. In our own time the Italian fascists took the year of Mussolini's march on Rome, instead of the Nativity of Christ, for the year One — the kind of thing for which they found a precedent in the French Republican Calendar. The Greek precedent suggests that the impulse to make a new start in history is a sign that something is amiss with society. When people proclaim that the past is not worth remembering and the present and future deserve to occupy all our attention, we can confidently look for a skeleton in the cupboard.

We are unique in one respect only — in science and technology, and this unprecedented technological development is producing some unintended effects which bring out certain enduring features of human nature: pollution, war, greed, and aggressiveness. We can't secure the survival of the human race unless we grapple with these, as the philosophers and religious teachers of past ages have long ago pointed out. The need for self-mastery, the need for limiting our greed is as relevant to our situation today as it was at the time of Socrates, the Hebrew prophets, and the Christian saints. They differ in their accounts of the facts, but in their telling us what we ought to do they are, I think, all agreed. This is a humbling thought — the fact that we have much greater material power only puts us in much greater danger to ourselves. This has been borne in on me by the experience of the last few years: It has made me more pessimistic and more conscious of the idiotic pride of the present-day world in thinking that we can jump clear of the limitations of human nature.

*   *   *

URBAN   There is, I believe, also a more intuitive side to our consciousness of our past which comes out clearly in your books: Your almost personal dialogues with the sounds and colors of history, the associative links that forge themselves in your mind at the sight of a landscape or a human gesture. The willows and poplars on the banks of the river Maritsa remind you of Hellenic Thrace and the entrenchment of the Ottoman Empire on the European side of the Straits; the foxskin caps of Bulgarian peasants you meet in a train remind you of the headgear in which Herodotus paraded the Asiatic Thracian contingent of Xerxes's expeditionary force, and so on.

TOYNBEE   My sensitiveness to the historic environment is part of living in the time dimension: It is a feeling for our ancestors and through our descendants, a feeling that we are trustees for the whole of human history. We have to hand down what has been handed down to us and see that it is preserved. Talking of *genius loci*: Traveling in the United States and other American countries I noticed that patches of the New World already have a history — in Virginia, the sites of the Civil War, for instance — whereas California and Colorado are almost historyless so far. The Rocky Mountains have no history in them, in the Allegheny Mountains there is a bit of history, in the mountains in New England there is much more. I felt the same in Brazil or Mexico: where there are sixteenth and seventeenth century buildings and the fields are several centuries old, I'm in my own world again. But then I go out to the Amazon forest, and it means nothing to me: This is a dramatic, striking landscape, but it is not embroidered with human actions and the memory of human actions. This is not a deliberate or self-conscious reaction on my part. It's a feeling for landscape as a scene of human events. Traveling by air and looking down on the pattern of fields, which is the same pattern in Indonesia, in Europe, and in America, I get the emotional sense of agricultural man's effect on the landscape of the planet. One glimpse at a landscape that one has studied in maps and books makes all the difference — you can't get that at second hand. I'm very conscious of this, and I always wanted to travel in countries where history has been made. I shouldn't be interested in traveling in historyless countries if there are such.

URBAN It isn't only that you connect things under the impact of landscape — it seems to me you bring together, in a variety of striking configurations, virtually all there is to be known about human affairs since the beginnings of recorded history.

For example, your annex to volume VIII of your *Study* (one of ten volumes and of ten lots of annexes) includes the following: "Optical Illusions in Hesiod's Vista of History"; "The Relativity of the Unit of Classification to the Object of Study"; "The Conflict of Cultures in the Soul of Solomós"; "The Peasant Majority of Mankind and the Agrarian Policy of the Soviet Union"; "The *Weltanschauung* of Alexander Herzen"; "Sicilian Light on Roman Origins"; "The Mercenary Soldier's Role as a Cultural Spearhead," and there are many others. How does all your information fall into place?

TOYNBEE It sorts itself quite naturally. I do have a card index of books and articles I have noted, but that is not really the source. I have notebooks on books I have read which I can use twenty or thirty years later. My wife says I have a sixth sense of knowing what note to make of something in a book which I shall need to use long afterward. I have a memory that makes it possible to pick out what I need. It's like a lot of rats and mice with their tails sticking out of a hole — I can pull them out by their tails. I haven't the whole rat or mouse present in my mind all the time, but I can fish him out for my purpose. It's something to do with my personal intellectual build, it's a form of omnivorous memory, like Jung's, who collected his instances from many, diverse sources. I feel a great kinship with this, although I didn't come across Jung's work until long after I had been working along similar lines myself.

URBAN   History, then, in the broad sense in which you use the word, is the unified study of human affairs.

TOYNBEE   I found I couldn't neglect any side. I am, regrettably, much worse equipped in some areas than in others — I'm poor in economics and in music, for instance. But where I feel confident in my competence, I try to do justice to all fields. Spengler's theory, with which I'm in sympathy, is that different civilizations have different major pursuits — the Faustian culture of the West had music as its major art, the Greeks had sculpture, and so on. He sees the relative importance of different sides of activity in different cultures — he sees the whole gamut of human relationships and accounts for the distinctive characters of civilizations rather plausibly by showing how they devoted different degrees of energy to different sides of life. But to be able to do that one has to know what these different sides were and that, once again, means studying human affairs as a whole.

URBAN   There is still an unanswered question at the back of my mind which takes us back to the beginning of this discussion. Eugène Ionesco described culture in a speech he made at the opening of the 1972 Salzburg Festival as "nothing but a screen which shelters us from our own fear of misery, of disgust, of sorrow, of fright, of death above all. . . . By expressing our misery in books we hoped to keep it at a distance."

With all due respect, isn't your *Study* a reaction to your fear of the senselessness of human affairs, of history being a mere catalogue (in the words of H. A. L. Fisher) of "one emergency following upon another," and ultimately of your fear

53

of death? Aren't your patterns, your rhythms, and your laws a psychological device to fend off chaos — to stamp some sense on a reality which you *know* to be profoundly meaningless?

If *I* were asked to put my cards on the table I would probably say that I regard all universal history as allegory; therefore my principal questions to an historian would be: What psychic factors drove him to write his history, and does his allegory come off? The truth of it is a minor matter.

TOYNBEE Human beings awake to consciousness to find themselves in a chaos. They then try to impose order on this chaos in order to make life endurable. Theology, nomothetic history, and, above all, the rituals for burial and for mourning, are so many attempts at this. We cannot verify whether the chart that we make of the mysterious universe corresponds to the elusive reality; but, in order to live, we have to make this chart, realizing it is an act of faith which is also an act of self-preservation.

patterns

URBAN I now suggest that we look at some of the laws, rhythms, and patterns you discern in history to see whether they are active in our own time and — more controversial — whether we can use them for making predictions, bearing in mind Namier's warning of the dangers of "juggling with uncorrelated precedents and analogies" and the special hazards of prophesying about living civilizations. First, challenge and response. You say that civilizations come into being under adverse conditions, that "soft" countries are less conducive to the rise of civilizations than "hard countries" whose growth and florescence are helped forward by "blows," "pressures," and "penalizations," and you mention as one example the hard physical environment of the Yellow River, which produced Chinese civilization, and the softer conditions on the Yangtse, which didn't produce one. You then ask yourself: How great has the pressure to be to be effective? And you answer, the most stimulating challenge is to be found in a mean between a deficiency of severity and an excess of it. If one were to translate these observations into practical policies — and as we are talking of laws we should perhaps be able to do that with some measure of assurance — how do we hit upon the right mixture? There are obviously challenges of salutary severity that stimulate, and there are those of overwhelming severity that kill.

TOYNBEE This raises the question of the possibility of prediction. Could one — seeing a society exposed to a certain challenge or irritant — forecast either that this stimulus will be insufficient to stir it to creative response or so severe that it will just wilt and collapse under the pressure? I don't myself believe one can forecast that a particular strength or type of stimulus will or will not produce the optimum conditions for creativity. One can see in retrospect that a particular stimulus — of which one may possibly measure the degree — has either produced a creative effect, or has been too overwhelming, or too slight. But I don't think one can apply this past experience, even if one can accumulate a large number of examples of it, to the future and make predictions on the strength of it. Our knowledge of the "variables" will never be complete enough.

URBAN Didn't Pieter Geyl challenge you on this point in a celebrated radio discussion? He was skeptical whether the birth of civilizations could be explained as a human response to a challenge from physical nature.

TOYNBEE Yes, he did. He took up the point apropos of the history of the Netherlands, and he maintained that the challenge of the landscape — reclaiming the land from the sea — was not central to the history of the development of the Netherlands. I should like to see what other Dutch historians say about Geyl's point. Geyl was a close friend of mine. He liked to be paradoxical, he loved to differ. He liked being friends with me, but he also half wished that I would fight back, and he was rather flummoxed when I refused. He was a very lovable man.

URBAN The observation you apply to the genesis of civilizations is tersely put in Goethe's famous stanza:

Wer nie sein Brot mit Tränen ass,
Wer nie die kummervollen Nächte,
Auf seinem Bette weinend sass,
Der kennt euch nicht ihr himmlischen Mächte!

But this doesn't seem to tell us any more about the right "mix" than your theory that civilizations "responded to drought and flood and swamp and thicket." What we are trying to find is the golden mean between the kind of swamp that makes a nonswimmer swim and the kind that drowns him.

TOYNBEE One example that comes to mind is the rise and decline of modern classical music, which is really German music. It coincides, in both German political history and economic history, with a period of adversity. It began with the generation after the Thirty Years War, which set Germany back economically and politically for a century or two, and it ended perhaps with Brahms, with the generation that saw the foundation of the second German Reich and the great economic boom that followed it in the latter part of the nineteenth century. Brahms died in 1897, and we might take him symbolically as perhaps the last outstanding representative of the great German classical composers. I do not think the rise of classical music was accidental. One can explain it sociologically in the sense that in times of economic and political adversity human ability tends to go into fields where there is still an opening for ability to express itself in creative work.

URBAN Is there any evidence of this happening in science?

TOYNBEE There is no hard and fast evidence, but my guess is that such evidence may be forthcoming. The invention of the atomic weapon, and the almost exclusive enrollment of atomic scientists in government service under conditions of secrecy, is a turning point in the history of science. At the same time, the freedom of enquiry wherever a scientist's curiosity leads him, has been — anyway in the past — the key to fruitful discoveries. In the capitalist countries many big corporations apparently believe in this disinterested research — they give large sums of money to research institutes, but the conditions under which this support is given only very indirectly require the researchers to do work that is useful to that corporation's technology and profits. Now, I do feel that the development of technology is going to lead to more and more bureaucracy and less and less freedom on the part of the scientists who are working for technology, and this makes me wonder whether people with enquiring minds, and with this need for freedom to follow wherever their intellect leads them, may not be put off by physical science and technology, which were the exciting subjects up to, say, 1945, and may not go into different fields. The change might be rather expedient if they went into social studies, into practical social work, or philosophy and religion instead. So there might be some parallel here with German classical music flourishing in times when Germany was going through a series of hardships, politically and economically.

URBAN Supposing we had a tolerably clear idea of the kind of hardships that are creative: Would it be ethically right to set about creating them? Is one entitled to *will* certain useful calamities, or would you feel it to be wrong to work for these things but right to turn them to our cultural account once they have happened outside our control?

TOYNBEE This is the *felix culpa* effect applied from theology to secular human life. As with *felix culpa,* if one were omnipotent and had to decide whether man should have a "fall" or not, it would be atrocious deliberately to cause him to fall, just as it would be atrocious deliberately to wish for the misery of unemployment, or decimation by warfare, in order to produce a challenge. But it may also be true that if these evils befall a civilization, the results may not be all negative. Very few people in nazi Germany or in Japan during the Second World War wished for the military defeat of Germany or Japan, but today I suppose most Germans and Japanese are gratified at the economic boom that has been a direct consequence of military defeat and the policy of the victors, and I should imagine they are also gratified that they have been freed from the despotism of the nazis and the militarism of the Japanese leadership.

Let me take this question on a wider ground: the prospects of Western civilization. The present distinctive feature of the West is wealth produced by the systematic application of science and technology in the service of greed, which is a universal human characteristic. But people are beginning to see that this scientifically gratified greed is going to be self-defeating. It's going to produce — short of atomic war — pollution and the exhaustion of resources. It may well be that the salvation of the Western world, and of the world in general, lies in some very great disasters which would reduce the material standard of living of the Western world as a whole. Maybe the human race can only survive through a kind of monastic attitude toward life — the Buddha's attitude and the attitude of the Christian saints — rather than the advertiser's attitude. Expansion must have its limits. Recent advances of astronomy and space exploration have shown that for practical purposes the habitat and resources of mankind are confined — and are going to be confined as far as we can see ahead — to this planet, and this planet's resources are not inexhaustible. Until quite lately the area of the planet was thought to be boundless. Circumnavigation was a very recent event, and the power of technology to exhaust the planet's irreplaceable resources, such as metals and mineral oils, was derisory. But now that we have occupied the whole usable area of the planet, it's quite possible that we may exhaust these resources. Owing to the advance of medical science we are having a vast increase of population, and the problem of living within our means is going to be inexorable. Now, the whole attitude of mind of present-day man is quite contrary to this. This is alarming. Our whole feeling is that we must expand — that our real income has to increase. The economically backward countries are feeling that they must reach the material standard of living of the developed world. Clearly, this is going to be impossible. With the world's population increasing, the average material standard of living is bound to fall. The only way in which we can prevent catastrophe is austerity. So we are back at the fact that the teachings of the higher religions for self-control, for putting the spirit before matter, were never more relevant than they are today and never more contrary to the state of mind of men than they are today.

URBAN At the risk of sounding brazenly cynical, the disasters you fear would surely take care of the population explosion and put the whole of mankind in a state of *felix culpa* with its fertile challenge to humanity to create new civilizations. One need not deliberately do anything for this to happen, nor even wish it to happen — probably all we'd have to do is to let the trends you have described run their course.

TOYNBEE It is true that, in the past, the catastrophic eclipses of old civilizations have sometimes been followed by the rise of new ones. But then, in the past, mankind lacked the power to do anything overwhelming — either good or evil. Today, we have the power to make the biosphere that coats the surface of this planet uninhabitable. We have the power to put an end to history and, indeed, an end to life. For this reason, I think we cannot afford to let ourselves fall over the edge of the precipice.

*   *   *

URBAN Your interpretation of the meaning of the Marxist attack on Christianity is perhaps another aspect of the austerity which you say the world will need in the coming decades. You argue that the Marxist challenge is not directed against the primitive Christianity of the third and fourth centuries — when some Christian communities lived in a state of frugality and consumer-communism — but that it challenges only the deformation of Christianity in the nineteenth and twentieth centuries. This, you write, is "a challenge to the living generation of Christians to examine their consciences and go back to an essential Christian activity. In that case history may record that the reawakening of the Christian conscience has been the one great practical achievement of Marx."

61

TOYNBEE I think the flaw in the Marxist critique of Christianity is a sin of omission rather than a sin of commission. Marxism is an excerpt from the Christian idea of socialism. Christians believe that all men are brothers because they are children of the same father, but they also believe that the brotherhood of man is impossible for us to achieve on this earth alone. According to Christian thinking, the brotherhood of man is only achieved by man enrolling himself as a citizen of the *Civitas Dei* which transcends the human world. Now, if you hold this belief, then you will also feel certain that the Marxian excerpt from Christian socialism must fail because it has deprived itself of the spiritual power which alone can make socialism a success. I may be permitted to use here the words I used in my *Study*: "The Christian critic will have no quarrel with the Marxian Socialism for going as far as it does: he will criticize it for not going far enough." In other words, Marxist socialism is a socialism manqué and is therefore doomed, but it does pose a challenge on which Christianity can rejuvenate itself and go back to its early inspiration — to austerity, the monastic life and the elevation of the spirit over material rapacity — which, as I have said, may well be our sole guarantees of survival as far as our terrestrial life and institutions are concerned.

URBAN Why do you say that Marxism is without spiritual power? The doctrine may well be, but in practice Marxism has inspired communists to very frugal living and outstandingly selfless conduct both in the communist countries and elsewhere.

TOYNBEE The weakness of Marxism is that it does nothing for the individual. Everyone has to face death and bereavement, a consciousness of his own inadequacy, errors of deed and judgment, and a host of other personal problems. For every human being the personal successes and failures of life are the things that really matter, as you can see from the news coverage of the popular press in any country. Public affairs are a kind of luxury — most people are unconscious of them. Now, to be told that the socialist state has the right to claim the individual's whole attention and all his loyalties because it is a higher form of human existence, is irrelevant to the individual's personal problems. If you look at the higher religions and philosophies you'll find that they have all done something for the individual — the salvation of the human soul is at the center of their concerns. Buddhism, like Marxism, is atheistic, on the other hand it is very greatly concerned with the problems of the individual. Confucianism, too, is almost entirely concerned with the human being's relations with other human beings — not public life in the abstract — and with personal relations radiating out into political relations by analogy. Now this concern with the individual soul is the all-important missing element in Marxism, and it is this giving something to the individual that explains the hold of the traditional religions and philosophies on human beings. Marxism, fascism, and nazism entirely lack this concern with personal salvation, and this is their greatest weakness, in the long view anyway.

URBAN Is it, do you think, possible that Marxism will add this element to its life-philosophy, not by causing Christianity to go back to its original inspiration, but by taking the individual under the umbrella of its own concerns? In Eastern Europe the rising crime rate, hooliganism, and the moral disorientation of youth have already raised a cry for the introduction of "ethics" in the school curriculum. It may not be long before "ethics" acquires an eschatological dimension, as in fact it did, to some extent, in 1967-68, in the philosophical writings of some Czechoslovak reform-Marxists, especially those involved in the Christian-Marxist dialogue. After all, Stalinism and Maoism have clothed Marxism with an aura of sham religiosity. Mightn't there arise in the ranks of the communists a John Ball, a Hans Hut, Taborite or Anabaptist prophets, so to speak, in reverse; seeing that egalitarianism and the community of goods are already established in the modern communist state (in theory, at any rate), they might want to give Marxism a spiritual dimension of the kind that satisfies the needs of the individual? A revivalist hippie culture, perhaps, rising against a background of official communism rather than western capitalism? An Anacommunism?

TOYNBEE I have no doubt that the call of some kind of religion that appeals to the individual and professes that it can solve his personal problems continues to be very real in the communist countries. However, I think this will probably take place outside the framework of Marxism. The communist regimes might disapprove of this almost as much as they would anathemize the kind of heresy you have in mind, but they might find themselves powerless to counteract it, rather as the Roman government found itself in the long run powerless to counteract Christianity. I don't myself believe that Marxism, even the young Marx's Marxism, is open enough to invite a spiritual revision (for it would have to be far more than a rejuvenation) of the kind you describe. But it is quite possible that there will be a demand for the open and positive coexistence of Marxism and religion. The people who went in for this personal religion might say, "We're good Marxists, we carry out the precepts of Marxism, but this is a field Marxism doesn't cover — we feel that this personal religion is necessary for us and we're going to have it." The Marxist regimes might say that this is a threat to their survival, and they might try to persecute it in the Roman Empire's way. But there is a great gap in Marxism's professedly self-sufficient philosophy of life, and my conjecture is that the gap will be filled outside the system, and it will be very hard for the system to do anything about it. A "Taborite" type of egalitarianism inside the system — and in some ways Maoism has the makings of that — would, of course, be even harder to combat, and if I were in the Soviet leaders' shoes, that is the one I would fear most. I think they do. At the same time, I don't think it would answer the religious problem of the individual.

*   *   *

URBAN It seems to me that your advice to Christians to rejuvenate their faith by going back to a distant phase in their history cannot be reconciled with your conception of "renaissances" — a law you have inferred from your study of the evocation of dead cultures by the living representatives of civilizations that are still going concerns. You argue that the proper label for this kind of historical event is not "Renaissance" but "renaissances" because there have been renaissances — literary, artistic, legal, political, institutional, philosophical, religious — other than the one to which we customarily attach the label Renaissance, and that they occurred not only in Orthodox Christendom and Western Christendom but also in the Hindu and Chinese civilizations. You call these evocations of a dead past "the raising of a ghost by the necromancer," and you leave little doubt in our minds that these resuscitated pasts and the living present don't mesh. You show that this "black art" is sterile, for the necromancer seldom "avoids or escapes the nemesis of being enslaved by a ghost that he has reanimated." And, significantly, you end your examination of renaissances with the words spoken to Odysseus by the shade of Achilles:

I would rather be a wretched peasant on the land, labouring as a serf with poor portionless man as my master, than be sovereign lord of all the legions of the shades of the dead and departed.

I would tend to label the rejuvenation of Christianity which you advocate a "renaissance," and I am not sure that we can, if we go along with what you say about "renaissances," expect it to be successful.

TOYNBEE This raises the question of minorities and establishments. From the sociological point of view the great and crucial event in the history of Christianity was its change-over from being the religion of a minority exposed to persecution — and therefore under a great challenge, and its membership selected under this challenge — to being the religion of the establishment which caused every self-seeking person to jump on to its bandwagon. In the nineteenth century, when Marx was attacking it, the inadequacy of Christianity as the religion of the establishment was particularly evident because it was doing nothing for the new industrial working class (even though this inadequacy was recognized in various papal encyclicals). But I think this was inherent in Christianity's position from the moment it became the religion of the establishment. The question is, can the spiritual characteristics of a religion which started as a persecuted minority, and which gained its characteristics from this, survive the apparent success of becoming the establishment religion. For being an establishment religion involves not being on the side of the angels but on the side of the big battalions, and it means accepting all the accretions that were originally alien to the religion.

URBAN *Is* such a rejuvenation likely in our conditions?

TOYNBEE In the history of Christianity the Quakers — the Society of Friends — have come the nearest that I know, but, of course, they have remained a minority (they were originally a rather persecuted minority). They have become a very affluent minority, but this has not corrupted them: They spend an enormous amount of their wealth and, what is more important, their spiritual energy in trying to do socially beneficient work. But still, they have not become characteristic — this piece of leaven has only very slightly leavened the lump.

URBAN There are, nevertheless, some signs — though they are far from being unanimous — that hardships and disestablishment can rejuvenate Christianity, even to the extent of making it go some way toward the austerity of the primitive Christian communities. The development of Christian thinking in some of the East European, communist countries would point in that direction. Are there any precedents for renaissances of this kind outside Christianity?

TOYNBEE Very few. In Islam there have been various militant, puritanical movements trying to go back to the religion of the Prophet, but though I have a great deal of sympathy with Islam — and no sympathy with the Christian denigration of Islam — I don't think that the militancy of Muhammad (I'm reminded of the massacre of Jewish husbandmen at Medina in A.D. 627 which he instigated) is a happy element in his career or in his bequest to posterity. Revivals like the Wahhabi movement are rather unfortunate returns to the original.

URBAN The problem whether Christianity has retained the power of self-renewal is central to your *Study*. You show that the place vacated by Christianity in our civilization is easily usurped by sham religions — paganisms: fascist worshippers of the state, communist worshippers of class, and so on. The spirit of man, you write, abhors a vacuum, and that is why it will seize upon any spiritual food rather than remain without sustenance. But although your description of the usurpation of the place of Christianity by modern paganisms is gloomy, in the last volume of your *Study* you seem to intimate that Christianity still has the power to release man from the grip of these modern paganisms and to offer him a higher alternative.

TOYNBEE I would say the paganisms have grown in number since the passages to which you refer were written, and there is no sign yet that people are disillusioned with them. At the same time there is disillusionment with the modern way of life. The facts are well known: Everybody has a car. Higher wages are canceled out by inflation. The wage earner brings home fabulous amounts of anyway nominal money in his weekly pay packet, but his week's work is odious to him compared to the work of the farmer. So in many ways the affluent — the officially successful — minority of the world is stultifying itself and becoming disillusioned. And then, as we have already seen, we are coming up against this death's head of the pollution of our habitat and the exhaustion of irreplaceable resources. The logical conclusion from all this is that we ought to follow out the precepts of the higher religions, but there is no sign at present that the mass of people would want to act in that direction — they are still going in the opposite direction. Is there going to be some disaster which will cause a big revulsion of feeling about the priorities in life and the relative values of things? I'm afraid nothing else is likely to have any real impact on us. I have become very pessimistic on this score, realizing the unteachability of human nature or, at any rate, the extremely slow rate at which human nature learns very obvious lessons. But we can't afford to be slow because technology is forcing the pace. I'm not saying it is impossible to learn from our mistakes. People have, from time to time, learned from history — the European Economic Community is one such example, but it is quite possible that, although we are aware of the lessons we ought to learn from history, we may refuse to act on that information. Like alcoholics or drug addicts, we know that we are going to our destruction, but the habit has us in its grip.

There is also an element of conscious resistance, especially in the young generations, to accept the experiences of earlier generations. In a sense this resistance against being indoctrinated is healthier than taking things on trust. But if you take nothing on trust you will make the same costly experiments in your own life as others made before you, and you will reap the same tragic results. History is predominantly the story of unlearned lessons. Mind you, sometimes the lessons have been learned too well. For example, since Joan of Arc the English have been very shy of continental commitments. They were frightfully shy of trying to conquer a European empire, but in the totally different situation of joining or not joining the European Economic Community this reaction is not rational. This is the negative side of over-learning a lesson. There can also be a positive side: Ever since we cut off King Charles's head and had a government of major-generals in consequence, we have stood for moderation in our domestic political life. But all these are long-range reactions — our problem is, as I say, that we can't afford to be slow, and I am not at all hopeful that our ability to respond will keep pace with the challenge of technology.

URBAN Let me approach this problem from a different point of view. We are still trying to answer the question: Has Christianity got the power in it to rejuvenate itself? And I propose to look at it now by using your concept of "creative minorities."

Not so many years ago it was respectable enough to talk of the role of elites in advancing societies from a primitive state to civilization. I think even now not many would disagree with you that it is the creative individual or the creative group of individuals, who, from time to time, forge ahead of the rank and file of society to answer some challenge that has been presented to the whole of society, but to which the majority of society were unresponsive. You claim that these creative minorities distinguish themselves by breaking contact with the rank and file, but once the challenge has been answered, they re-enter into contact with the majority. Now, I'm trying to test this thesis against current experiences: Would you say we are going through a phase in which the creative elites have gone into hibernation? Would you think of Christianity in terms of an establishment elite which has gone into voluntary psychic exile so that it may — its faith purified of accretions — re-enter the world as a truly creative minority?

TOYNBEE I think it is possible, and it is, of course, one of my hopes. But if an elite of this kind were to return, it might do so in a form unrecognizable to the traditional orthodox in the sense that if the leaders of this return movement were examined in orthodoxy — "Do you believe in articles 1,2,3,4, etc. of the Creed?" — they would be faulted every time. Nevertheless, *they* would be the genuine new leaders of a new Christianity. This may be wishful thinking on my part, but, as far as I can be objective about this, I do think this return after a renewal is a possibility.

*　　*　　*

URBAN Next I propose to look at your discussion of militarism in Sparta to see whether the self-destruction of the Lycurgean system has any relevance to our understanding of Soviet militarism.

You quote in the third volume of your *Study* Aristotle's epitaph on Spartan militarism.

Peoples ought not to train themselves in the art of war with an eye to subjugating neighbours who do not deserve to be subjugated. . . . The paramount aim of any social system should be to frame military institutions, like all its other institutions, with an eye to the circumstances of peace-time, when the soldier is off duty; and this proposition is borne out by the facts of experience. For militaristic states are apt to survive only so long as they remain at war, while they go to ruin as soon as they have finished making their conquests. . . .

You add to these observations that the Spartan tradition died hard: It continued to be practised out of sheer conservatism for nearly two centuries after Messenia had been lost.

One frame of reference that describes the Soviet system rather better than most is that of the "mobilization state." It denotes the siege mentality in which the citizens of the Soviet Union have been living since the 1917 revolution — the mobilization of the citizenry for a great proliferation of "campaigns," "battles," and "victories." Of course, the siege mentality is as old as the history of despotism, but in Russia it has been practised with a totalitarian consistency which is second perhaps only to the rigors of the Lycurgean militarism itself. Other parallels also spring to mind. You describe in your book the criminality of the Spartan "Secret Police" "in order that the tiny minority of Spartiate 'Peers' might keep their feet on the necks of a numerically overwhelming majority of 'inferiors' and 'Dependants' and 'New Members.'" The Soviet parallel to these would be the class enemy, the non-Russian nationalities, and the satellite states. More relevant still, because it is prophetic of the Katyn massacre of Polish officers (and perhaps also of the failure, through Soviet inactivity, of the Warsaw uprising), is the assassination of the Helots who had volunteered to serve with the Spartan forces in the Atheno-Peloponnesian war (of 431-404 B.C.). This is described by Thucydides:

The whole policy of the Spartans towards the Helots is governed by considerations of security. . . . They proclaimed that all Helots who could show a distinguished war record should present themselves for selection to receive their freedom. This was simply a trap — the calculation being that those Helots who considered that they had the best claim to liberation would be just the helots who would have the spirit to take the initiative in falling upon their masters. So they selected two thousand of them; and these two thousand gave thanksgivings for their manumission by crowning themselves with garlands and visiting the shrines of the Gods in procession. But the Spartans were not long in making away with them — and this with such secrecy that nobody ever knew how each of the victims had met his end.

TOYNBEE This was indeed sounding the darkest depths of human conduct and prophetic, as you say, of the treachery of Katyn, the common denominator being the oligarchy's — justified — fear of the "serfs" who, as Xenophon observes of some Spartan conspirators, "would be delighted to eat them alive."

Now, I believe the mobilization mentality in the Soviet Union is not strictly comparable with Spartan militarism, for the latter was designed to hold down large, conquered territories which a numerically inferior Sparta would otherwise have found it very difficult to hold down. When we speak of Soviet militarism, we mean it more metaphorically, in the sense that the Soviet government uses military types of techniques and military language for mobilizing national resources. Of course, every now and then this overlaps into militarism of the traditional kind, but I believe this is not its main function. You mentioned siege mentality — I think Russia has had a siege mentality for a very long time, far longer than the communist regime. In the fifteenth century, after the fall of Constantinople, Russia was the only independent Eastern Orthodox Christian country left, and a great part of Russia had been conquered by Poland and Lithuania which were Western Catholic countries. Already the Russians were conscious of being the citadel of orthodoxy. Why did Peter the Great westernize Russia in his drastic way technologically? The reason was, again, the siege mentality, because Poland and Sweden — second class Western powers — had proved themselves much stronger in military technology than Russia. Why did the Bolsheviks, as soon as they came to power, go in for a vast program of technological modernization? Because in 1905 Japan had given Russia a very great shock, and in the First World War Russia had been proved to be technologically utterly backward, not only compared to her allies, but compared to Germany, of course. So I think this siege mentality is probably the key to the Soviet "mobilization state," and my point would be that this is independent of the particular communist ideology which is, really, just the most recent form of Russian ideology. Whether Russian ideology was that of Peter the Great, who headed a contemporary, enlightened, westernized monarchy, or of Ivan the Terrible, who copied an earlier model of Western despotism, the siege mentality — the idea of keeping the country in a state of permanent mobilization — was common to both.

URBAN I would perhaps give more emphasis to the old-fashioned, militaristic element in the Soviet siege mentality. Remembering Russia's anxious and swift military reaction to East Berlin in 1953, to Hungary in 1956, and to Czechoslovakia in 1968, and the Soviet government's long-standing desire to legitimize its grip on Eastern Europe by a security treaty, I feel that Soviet military power as a means of holding down Russia's satellites — and, of course, also as a symbol of her status as a superpower — has become almost self-justificatory and is less and less an expression of technological inferiority, especially as this inferiority is, by all accounts, fast disappearing.

TOYNBEE Obviously the Russian regime acts on the assumption that Russia is under great pressure. I think there *is* pressure — rising pressure, too — from the subject East European countries and from that half of the Soviet population which isn't Great Russian and which is increasing faster than the Great Russian population. Nevertheless, the chief pressure the Russians are conscious of is economic and technological competition with the West and Japan. Their terrible fear is that, once again, they may be out-distanced technologically by part of the outer world and therefore be at the mercy of the West or of Japan or both. The history of Soviet economic and technological espionage and counterespionage certainly points in that direction. It is, I think, this, more than the literally military necessity of holding down the subject peoples, that causes the Soviet regime to enforce the mobilization mentality and to practice mobilization.

URBAN To understand the Soviet regime's mobilization mentality, I think one has also to understand the social and psychological background which makes Russian governments oppress other

73

nations, or which makes it at least possible for Russian governments to do so. Would you subscribe to Lenin's judgement that "the century-long history of the repression of the movements of the oppressed nations, and the systematic propaganda in favor of such repression by the upper classes, have created in the Great-Russian people prejudices, etc., which are enormous obstacles to the cause of its own liberty"? I am personally more inclined to turn this round and say that a people which is not free is more likely to be used to oppress others, whether under the banner of a Holy Alliance or some totalitarian Messianism.

TOYNBEE In the nineteenth century there was a very limited educated public in Russia, and its political influence was smaller still. Nevertheless, I've seen it said that in 1878 it was this very limited public opinion — what Lenin calls the "upper classes" — that forced the Tsarist government to make war on Turkey. The government was unpopular with a growing number of educated people. The Decembrist revolution in 1825 had given a foretaste of the strength of Slavophile liberalism. Alexander II felt that he could not afford to go against this chauvinism. These Russian idealists, who claimed to discover Russia's peculiarity in the socialistic soul of Russia and rejected the individualist Western soul, worried the Tsarist regime a great deal more than Herzen, Belinsky, and Bakunin who revolted against the Slavophile doctrine. Later, when the Duma was established not so long before the breakdown of Tsardom, the Duma turned out to be more chauvinistic, in trying to incorporate Finland fully into the Russian empire, than the Tsarist regime had ever been. The Tsarist regime was rather liberal toward Finland. There was a kind of personal union between the two countries; the Tsar was Grand Duke of Finland, and Alexander III, who had a personal liking for the Finns, was able to resist the demands of Russian nationalists for the abolition of Finnish autonomy. There was no Russification. But the Duma insisted on Russification, and the Tsarist government had to appease it, so that in 1910 responsibility for all important Finnish legislation was transferred to the Duma. In other words, from the Finnish point of view it was the educated upper class — the Duma — rather than the Tsar, who was the villain of Russian imperialism. And this would endorse Lenin's point. It also illustrates one weakness of autocracy that even autocracies, precisely because they are unpopular and uncertain of their position, have to conciliate public opinion, as far as public opinion of any potency exists, especially if the conciliation can be done by the relatively undangerous device of adding to the alienation of an already alienated foreign dependency.

On the Polish question, too, the nineteenth century liberals and intellectuals in Russia (Pushkin among them) were surprisingly imperialistic and chauvinistic, and in the Russian novels of the period Poles were always caricatured, guyed, treated with obvious hostility even by the most enlightened Russian writers. As the Russian intelligentsia couldn't be free at home, they compensated psychologically for this unfreedom by being all for the oppression of non-Russian subjects, and as the Russian government was repressing Russians successfully it didn't take so much to repress other peoples as well. The large and illiterate peasant masses went along with this (as they always do) with, I think, a considerable degree of Schadenfreude, giving the Poles (and in 1849 the Hungarians) as good as they were receiving from their masters.

I'm not arguing that these are Russian racial characteristics. The siege mentality goes back only as far as the Mongol conquest and domination. Pre-Mongol Russia was very different, it was much more open to the world. If you look at dynastic history, the pre-Mongol Russian rulers married not only into Byzantine imperial families but into all the royal families of Western Europe. Russian traders went to Constantinople and to Western Europe — it was an open society. Then, as she had begun to shake off the Mongol yoke, Russia suddenly closed, not only in response to the end of Mongol domination but also because all other Orthodox Christian countries had been conquered by the Turks and (as I mentioned earlier in this discussion) Russia was left alone as the solitary Orthodox independent country, under pressure from Turks and from Western Christians.

URBAN The post-Mongolian character of Russia would, then, explain the distortions which Marxism suffered when it landed in Russian, rather than German or British hands.

TOYNBEE Yes — Stalin was a Georgian and an orthodox Christian seminarist at one stage. This tells us something. Trotsky, on the other hand, was a Jew; he was brought up in Southern Russia — he had much wider horizons.

URBAN Let me ask you a speculative question: Supposing the Russian revolution had been followed by communist revolutions in Germany, France, and England soon after the First World War, would the specific gravities of these nations have asserted themselves in the resulting communist regimes, just as characteristically as the Byzantine tradition of Russia has shaped the Soviet variety of Marxist communism?

TOYNBEE I think so — as in Russia, they would have become moulded by past tradition. The weight of past traditions is very great, and revolutionists always have the illusion that they can make a clean break, jump clear of the past. They are nearly always disappointed.

De Tocqueville showed in his *L'Ancien Régime et la Révolution* that revolutions do not represent a break with the past — in fact, it is the *ancien régime* that is realized all over again by the revolution. The history of Buddhism in China is one good example: The Chinese were converted to Buddhism, but they turned Buddhism into something utterly Chinese which Ceylonese or Burmese Buddhists wouldn't recognize as being Buddhism. The Chinese are doing the same with communism, and the Russians have done the same with communism. I'm convinced that the French and the British would have done likewise. In fact, French and Italian communism today is already very different not only from Russian communism but also from what Marx himself would have wished. The French and the Italian communists had to adapt themselves to the past traditions of their country. It's the price they had to pay for ceasing to be an underground movement and becoming official.

URBAN What sort of form would communism have taken in Britain? Would the communists have abolished Parliament and the Monarchy?

TOYNBEE Marx believed that Britain was destined to be the first communist country, and from the point of view of his theory that was quite logical, as Britain was the first industrialized country.

URBAN But even Marx, slightly to Lenin's chagrin, dismissed any idea that a British revolution would smash the "ready-made state machine." Writing in 1871, Marx thought that Britain was without a militaristic clique, and to a large extent without a French type of bureaucracy, and that for these reasons a people's revolution in Britain would be possible without making it necessary to destroy the existing order.

TOYNBEE And I believe Marx had the better judgment, because Lenin's later outburst that Britain (and America) had sunk into the "all-European filthy, bloody morass of bureaucratic-military institutions which . . . suppress everything," made Britain, too, appear ripe for the smashing and destruction for which she wasn't ripe, for in 1917 Lenin misread the nature of British society and British institutions. A British revolution would have been a caricature in its moderation and half-heartedness. It would have had as its symbol the British policeman's rounded helmet rather than the spiked helmet of the Prussian military or the whip of the Russian police. The basic indifference of the British public would have rubbed off the edges of any revolution. It would have disgusted not only Lenin and Stalin but Marx as well. Abolish the Monarchy? I don't know. Wouldn't the British revolutionists have decided rather that the Monarchy was a useful, convenient instrument and have regarded it even with some pity and have spared it? It would have given them instant legitimacy (rather on the post-Second World War Japanese pattern) — the thing communist regimes find it hardest to come by where revolutions have completely destroyed the social order.

I met an American some years ago who had watched, on a Sunday afternoon, some communist speakers address a crowd from Nelson's monument in Trafalgar Square. There was an Englishman standing next to him. "That *is* a good point," he said to the American, "I'm not a communist but he is making a very strong case, isn't he?" He was making a purely professional, a kind of aesthetic judgement of the communist speaker's capability. Now, this astonished the American — how could he be so detached? And this is the sort of mentality that would prove fatal for British communism. Can there be a more comic spectacle than a British communist demonstration being tamely shepherded by unarmed policemen to make sure that no one interferes with it and the traffic isn't unduly disrupted? If a communist party can allow that to happen, its claim to be the revolutionary force of our time is rather compromised.

Alexander Herzen was in Switzerland at the end of 1848, watching the refugees streaming in from the countries where the revolution had failed in Western Europe, and in his memoirs he speaks of these revolutions with undisguised contempt. Of course, he says, these Western revolutions are absurd. They aren't serious. When we in Russia make a revolution, it'll be the real thing — this is the brunt of his comments. One can imagine what he would have thought of a British type of revolution or the deportment of the British Communist Party.

URBAN Herzen, although a fervent westernizing socialist, shared some of his Slavophile liberal compatriots' faith in Russian destiny as a force that would perhaps save the West from its bourgeois scruples, from its stagnation, from its traditions, from its paralysis which, he says, deprive "the Western European of the use of half his limbs." Now in the fifth volume of your *Study* there is a significant quotation from Macaulay's essay *History* in which Macaulay castigates the petrifaction of the Roman Empire, arguing that the barbarian invasions were a blessing in the long term because they broke up Rome's petrifaction: "It cost Europe a thousand years of barbarism to escape the fate of China." If you put this side by side with Herzen's emphasis on the Russian character, its irrationality, its lack of scruples, its "naturalness" and "tough muscles," would you say that the Soviet embodiment of this uninhibited Russia is the force that might save bourgeois Europe from its present degeneracy? Do you expect Russia to act as a brutal but effective rejuvenator of a West that has lost faith in itself?

TOYNBEE I cannot see Brezhnev's Russia rejuvenating Europe, for this is certainly not Herzen's Russia, or the Slavophile liberals' Russia, but a latter-day Tsarism with its police mentality, bureaucracy, and siege reflexes all taken over intact. The siege reflex alone would rule out any analogy with the barbarian invasion of Rome. China may be a different matter. If (as we discussed a minute ago) Soviet Russia were a true spearhead of Marxism, then it might help Western Christianity to find its way back to its sources. But the Soviet system isn't a Marxist state in the sense in which Marx would have wished it to be, so it is unlikely to act as a catalyst at this level either.

On Macaulay's general point — and he was anticipated on this by both Gibbon and Hume — there is, in the lives of civilizations, a balance between periods of strife, disintegration, and destructiveness, and periods of rally and retrenchment. This is one of the patterns I observe in history — I call the first a "Time of Troubles" and the second "Universal States." When you have disunity, political, military, or economic strife, you may get a very great release of spiritual energy, stimulus, liveliness. But then there comes a time when the destructive effect of chaos outweighs the stimulating effect of variety, of the absence of rules, of anarchy; when that stage is reached, society has to incapsulate itself for self-preservation in a "Universal State," even though the price of this may be bureaucratization, standardization, loss of creativity, and spiritual torpor. We can observe this pattern in the Greco-Roman world and the Roman empire, in the contending Chinese states and the Chinese empire, and so on. The ideal is to have a balance, but this is very hard to attain and very hard to maintain. I don't think Europe in the nineteenth century was suffering from the kind of spiritual degeneracy which Herzen attributed to European society — precisely perhaps *because* there was strife and chaos — nor does it seem likely to me that if Europe *were* heading for petrifaction in a "Universal State," an influx of Russian "barbarism" could stop it. It would make it worse.

*   *   *

URBAN In your classification of civilizations you regard Russia as part of the Byzantine civilization, distinct from our own. Has the history of this century confirmed you in the correctness of this distinction? You say repeatedly in your book that the First and Second World Wars were civil wars, implying that all contending parties belonged to the same civilization. Would a war between an expanding totalitarian Russia and a post-Christian West be a civil war too, or would it be a war between civilizations?

TOYNBEE The Byzantine countries have been subject to increasing degrees of Western influence in various forms for quite a long time. Communism itself is a left-handed form of Westernization. Peter the Great stood for the same thing. When the Greeks revolted against the Turks and appointed a Bavarian prince as their king, they were consciously Westernizing after having been very hostile to the West for centuries. And the same is true for all Byzantine countries. The point I make here is that through Westernization the whole world has been knit together in the rudiments of a single society, so that war between different parts of the world would be a civil war in the sense that the first two world wars were civil wars of the Western world. The world is a cultural and social and moral unity to a sufficient extent today to make it reasonable to call any war a fratricidal or civil war.

URBAN But even though the Second World War was a civil war, was it not a "just war" in the Christian sense? Didn't the positive evil of nazism make it into that?

TOYNBEE Yes, I suppose a fratricidal war can, at the same time, be a just war; it is a tragedy to have war between fellow human beings, but a just war is a legitimate conception in the sense that not to have that war would be a greater evil. I certainly felt during the Second World War — and with a lesser degree of intensity during the First World War — that these were just wars in the sense that to give in to imperial Germany or to Hitler's Germany would have been a greater evil. Of course, the war with Hitler was a domestic war inside the Western world. Although nazi Germany was a kind of apostate from the Western world, she still was a Western country with a Western past which she repudiated only temporarily. The relations of Russia with Western Europe and America are less intimate than were Germany's relations. Now that the whole world is knit together in one Westernizing society, a war with Stalin's Russia would have been a fratricidal war too, but less fratricidal, shall we say, than the war with Hitler. But both would have been just wars in my view.

URBAN The war against Hitler was a just war, even, I suppose, Stalin's war against Hitler. But out of Stalin's war issued a phenomenon which you describe time and again in your *Study:* the conqueror's intoxication with victory which, you say, eventually spells his ruin. You show how the victor's pride and predatory practices undermined the Spanish and Portuguese empires and the British empire after the conquest of Canada and Bengal. You say that the Indian Empire might never have been retained had Warren Hastings's impeachment and the 1784 India Bill not put an end to some of the East India Company's rapacity. How far are these judgements valid in our own time? Since the Second World War both Soviet and United States policies have been a mixture of missionary zeal and predatory practices. Both powers conquered enormous "empires" or spheres of influence; neither tolerated any threat to its military, political, or "ideological" security, although on the all-important point of how their respective interests were defended the analogy breaks down.

TOYNBEE The United States and the Soviet Union were the two principal victors of the war, and they both made the traditional mistakes of victors. Firstly, each acquired an empire after liquidating other nations' empires. The Americans have, in practice, acquired an East Asian empire which they are now finding too hot to hold, and the Russians acquired an East European empire. Secondly, as a pair of victors often has after previous wars, they fell out with each other and tried to enlist their defeated enemies on their respective sides. The Americans are already perhaps regretting these elementary mistakes and retreating from some of their earlier commitments. Whether the Russians will find the East European countries too hot to hold and be rather anxious to get out at some stage, I don't know. What is obvious is that America and Russia are both in adversity at present, and that Japan and Germany — the two principal defeated countries — are now prospering. This is ironical but not surprising.

Furthermore, neither the Americans nor — especially — the Russians reckoned with nationalism. The Americans at least did not have a philosophical commitment on this point, but the Russians were guided, nominally anyway, by Marx and Lenin, who thought that international class loyalties were stronger than nationalism and that communism would subordinate, or even eliminate, nationalism. This has been proved untrue: Stalin made Marxism an engine for Russian nationalism, and when China and Yugoslavia broke away from Russia, they destroyed the myth of monolithic communism for nationalistic reasons. My feeling is that the East European countries, too, are more concerned with keeping, or regaining, their national independence than with a particular kind of regime. If a communist leadership in any East European country were able to do what Tito did and shake off Russian control, the people of that country would gladly accept the communist regime, because nationalism is much more important to them than democracy. This makes life difficult for the Russians, but it doesn't bode well for the future of a united Europe either.

URBAN You don't think the old 1848 equation: Liberation equals liberalization, holds true, or is likely to hold true again, as the East European countries get more industrialized and sophisticated?

TOYNBEE I think I do, although it is hard to generalize. If liberation is fully achieved over a period of time, then liberalization might follow. But as long as a country lives under external pressure, or even under the possibility of external pressure, national solidarity — which is only one step away from nationalism — will have the first claim on its attention and energies. It's striking in Israel, since the cease fire after the one-week war, how internal strains and stresses — and these are, or can be, the makings of democracy — have come to the surface. As long as there was fighting and the Israelis lived in a state of mobilization, there was a monolithic solidarity among them. Now the differences between the European and non-European settlers, the differences among social classes, between labor and capital, have come into full view and full play because the external pressure has been removed. I am convinced the same would happen in Rumania or Poland if the Russian pressure were effectively removed from them.

URBAN Wouldn't this depend on the social and cultural sophistication of these countries — some moving much faster than others?

TOYNBEE As we well know, the Czechs would find it very easy to turn liberation into liberalization, as they did even under conditions of partial liberation in 1968, and the Hungarians and East Germans would be not far behind. The Poles, Rumanians, and Bulgarians might be slower, but among these, too, the Polish road to liberalization would be shorter than that of the two Balkan countries, despite the Poles' strong chauvinism.

URBAN Eastern Europe has now been under Soviet domination for a quarter of a century — much of it under direct Soviet occupation, and all of it under Soviet institutions. Yet the spiritual-cultural effect of this partnership has been virtually nil. It seems to me your assessment of the importance of the cultural element in the contact of civilizations explains very well why this has been so. In the fifth volume of your *Study* you tell us that the cultural element in a civilization is "its soul and life-blood and marrow and pith and essence and epitome, while the political and, *a fortiori,* the economic element are, by comparison, superficial and nonessential and trivial manifestations of a civilization's nature and vehicles of its activity. It is only in so far as it succeeds in radiating itself out on the cultural plane that a civilization can ever genuinely and completely assimilate an alien body social with which it has come into contact. . . ." The East European experience fits this description to perfection: The Soviet Union's hegemony over Eastern Europe has expressed itself, since 1947, in a great many important ways, but none, one may safely say, has touched the "soul and life-blood" of the East European nations. There has been no assimilation of the alien bodies social.

TOYNBEE Since about the year 1000, Hungary, Moravia, Bohemia, Poland, and part of Yugoslavia — Slovenia and Croatia — have been parts of Western Christendom. Today they are parts of, and regard themselves as belonging to, the modern Western world. Rumania, Serbia, and Bulgaria are, of course, like Russia, Eastern Orthodox Christian countries by origin who "received" Western civilization (I am using the word "received" in the sense in which we speak of the "reception" of Roman law). Now, the Rumanians, Serbs, and Bulgarians are extremely conscious that they received Western civilization rather *better* than the Russians. In other words, all these East European satellites of the Soviet Union feel themselves culturally superior to the Russians. You aren't influenced culturally by people whose cultural superiors you feel yourselves to be. Russia has been singularly unsuccessful, and she is bound to be, and will continue to be, unsuccessful in having any cultural impact on the East European countries, and without a cultural impact these countries will continue to be, so to speak, indigestible for Russia. For decades and decades Russia may dominate Eastern Europe militarily and politically, but Eastern Europe will emerge un-Russified.

But if you look in the other direction, at the Caucasus and Central Asia, inside the Soviet Union, you will find Russification is the key to modernization, to entering the great world, and to making a career. I would expect that even people like the Armenians, who have a very ancient and powerful civilization of their own, are influenced by Russification. I guess that this is attractive even for the culturally conscious and ambitious young Armenians and, *a fortiori,* it is attractive for the rather underdeveloped Central Asian peoples — Islam is backward looking and antediluvian. There is no question here of any feeling of cultural superiority toward the Russians; so, Eastward, Russification is successful, and Russian domination isn't effectively opposed.

URBAN I wonder to what extent the alleged cultural "superiority" of the East European countries may be due to the fact that they are small nations, and that they've been outside the mainstream of European culture. You make the interesting point in your book that the thinkers, poets, historians, and artists of large nations are easily misled into believing that they live in a culturally self-contained world. You mention the example of the French historian Jullian who "depicts a spiritual France which furnishes him with the experience of human life so exhaustively that, if the rest of the world were to be annihilated and France left solitary but intact, M. Jullian would perhaps hardly be sensible of any spiritual impoverishment."

You then argue that if one's habitat is a large and old nation such as France, the intellectual substitution of a nation for mankind is just possible, but it would be impossible to write the history of Western society round a state like Czechoslovakia or Yugoslavia, for they hardly have a national consciousness stretching back more than fifty years. "In contrast to France, Slovakia and Croatia fall so short of constituting historical universes in themselves that, when isolated, they cease to be intelligible."

It seems to me that the reverse side of the small size and periodic historical isolation of these nations is their massive cultural achievement. For, whereas a Frenchman or an Englishman or a German might be laboring under the illusion that he could find the history and culture of mankind encapsulated in his own nation, a Pole or Hungarian or Moravian couldn't begin to entertain such an idea. He would, rather, feel that he wasn't fully civilized until he had familiarized himself with the cultures and languages of other nations, and this would mean acquiring a consciousness of a "European" culture with its supranational horizons. It is certainly true that the Poles, Czechs, and Hungarians tend to look upon themselves — though not always upon each other — as the true vehicles of a universal European culture.

TOYNBEE The Poles are a good example. The constant partitions of Poland have made it almost inevitable that Poland should become a byword for nationalism. It is a joke among non-Poles who meet Poles that Poles can't keep Polish nationalism out of any conversation for any length of time, and the Poles themselves joke about this. At the same time it is true that the Poles are supranationalists in the sense of being citizens of the world, rather like the Jews: They lost their own country and they were scattered abroad.

At the beginning of the Second World War, I visited Paris, and I was taken by some Poles to the Polish library on one of the islands of the Seine. They pointed out wistfully that this was the only piece of Polish territory that had never been under foreign occupation — and, in a few months, it was under German occupation. But this illustrates the point that the same historical facts that caused Poland's political nationalism, also generated Polish cultural internationalism.

Nations that are on the geographical fringes of civilization often make great efforts to keep in touch with the center, while people in the center — the French or the modern British — do not. But the early English, after their conversion to Christianity, flocked to Rome as pilgrims. In the Borgo there was an English colony in the early Middle Ages. The Poles and Hungarians took care to learn other languages and to be in touch with the heart of the Western world. I remember questioning a Tirolese Austrian friend of mine about other parts of the Habsburg empire. But he was useless. "I've never traveled there," he said. "But surely you live at a stone's throw of, say, Slovenia," I answered. "Why should I go to Slovenia? When I have money I travel of course to the West, to Paris or Geneva or Brussels or somewhere like that."

URBAN I should imagine your popularity in the small countries — both in Eastern Europe and Western Europe — may have something to do with the same cultural universalism. Small nations, and minorities within larger nations, would derive a certain satisfaction from an approach to history which stresses cross-cultural and cross-national connections and doesn't allow the more powerful or successful nations to get away with telling the story. If history is told in terms of civilizations rather than nations, your numerical inferiority and fringe position do not matter so much.

TOYNBEE This is probably so. If you have — or if you recently have had — an assured national place in the world, as the French and the British have had, you may dislike this universalistic approach — it may be offensive to you. But if you are small, or defeated, or uprooted, you become, in consequence, a citizen of the world. Namier had an interesting observation about this. In his monograph on the 1848 revolution, he studied, in his typical way, the origins and careers of the 1848 German revolutionaries, and he found that most of them were inhabitants of territories that had changed their political allegiance in the settlement of 1814-15. They, or their parents, had been torn out of their traditional local loyalties, particularly the small German principalities, but they couldn't do without some kind of political allegiance. So they became pan-German nationalists instead. I'm sure this is true and it illuminates your point.

URBAN I think the same is true of the post-Second World War unifiers of Europe: of de Gasperi with his Austro-Hungarian, of Schumann with his Alsatian, of Adenauer with his Rhenish background —

TOYNBEE — and if one knew the Rheinland, it was a kind of Prussian colony, an East Pakistan to Potsdam. It is certainly true that if you're deprived of your traditional allegiance, you find a different one — probably a wider one — in compensation.

* * *

URBAN In 1493, as you point out in your *Study*, Spain and Portugal obtained the whole overseas world by a papal award to promote the Christian faith in the newly discovered territories. I'm struck by a possible parallel with the Chinese communist claim that Maoists are the appointed trustees of the underdeveloped world. It was Lin Piao who gave China this missionary interpretation of Marxism, and it is now axiomatic in China although Lin Piao has fallen from grace.

TOYNBEE I could see China putting herself at the head of this kind of movement — the ancestral gods of History having entrusted the colored poor to the care of the Middle Kingdom. But whether this claim can be made good will depend, to a large extent, on how far, in the next ten to twenty years, the industrialized Western countries can solve the problems of pollution and population, and whether they can devise better means for the husbandry of the world's nonreplenishable resources than they have done so far. If they cannot, there will probably be a strong reaction in the developing world against extreme industrialization, and this might make China's limited industrialization, Chinese frugality, and Chinese puritanism, positive examples which the rest of the developing world might wish to follow —

URBAN — assuming, of course, that developing countries are more willing to learn from the mistakes of the developed countries than the developed countries have been willing to learn from their own.

TOYNBEE Yes, I am, for the moment, assuming that, but I share your feeling that the nonteachability (or very slow teachability) of the human race is pretty universal. At the same time it is true that in Burma, for example, there is a definite policy now to adopt certain elementary sides of modern technology, public health, and so on, but not to go full out to catch up with the Western world in industrialization. The idea would seem to be to keep the traditional peasant way of life, supplemented selectively with modern gadgets.

URBAN I wonder whether the balance the Chinese have so far been able to maintain — or were, perhaps, forced to maintain since their break with Moscow — between agriculture and industry is due to Mao's personality. Mightn't the technocrats, after Mao's death, opt for the same sort of break-neck industrialization (with American or Russian help) which made both Japan and Russia great powers in a short time? The temptation would be great and the Confucian background might not be strong enough to hold the Chinese back even if they were persuaded (as I'm sure they are not) that the magnetism of their example for the third world is the balanced nature and unhurried speed of their industrialization. I don't think communists argue on those lines.

TOYNBEE   This is possible. It is possible because China was immensely humiliated from the Opium War until the communists took power, and, if you have been humiliated, you react by becoming aggressive. One feeling in China must be that China must have power in the modern sense. An enlightened Chinese might well say to himself: "All this modern technology is hateful, it sets our teeth on edge, and we have — just because it is aesthetically and psychologically hateful to us — waited for a century to go in for it when the Japanese did it immediately. But, in consequence, we have been kicked about by Japanese, by Europeans, by Americans — everybody — and our first priority must be to get even with the modern industrialized world." That is one possible reaction. The other possibility is that the Confucian point of view, which is essentially one of moderation and balance, rather like the Greek ideal — the golden mean which the Greeks never practiced — may prevail. After all, the Confucian attitude toward life is deeply rooted in China; it has first colored Chinese Buddhism and then Maoist communism, and it might color post-Maoism too. It will be a tug of war between these two tendencies. We must not underestimate the pull of the weight of past tradition, however strongly the Chinese may resent being treated as "natives" and may wish to show that they are not "natives." But whichever way the decision might go, it will be for national and traditional reasons and not because the Chinese communists would want to, or could, mount a deliberate campaign to prize loose the underdeveloped world from Soviet influence. But if they do settle for a balanced industrialization with very limited growth targets, they may well inherit the third world, in Lenin's sense, by offering the underdeveloped countries a middle-of-the-road example between the poverty of underdevelopment and the ravages of inordinate industrialization.

URBAN Where I see a danger is that the Confucian tradition — filial piety, the family conceived as a microcosm of society, the loyalty of the extended family, the educational awareness and frugality of the Chinese — might be so easily translated into a fully fledged, paternalistic, industrialized society rather on the Japanese model, with Japanese rates of pollution but without the freedom of the Japanese political system. In fact, China would be getting the worst of both worlds: great despoliation of the environment with no means of self-correction — a Japanese kind of efficiency painted red.

TOYNBEE This is a possibility — a rule of technocrats, with the state acting as Confucian paterfamilias, demanding and receiving, as you say, filial obedience from the workers. The extremism of the Cultural Revolution shows that Mao must have perceived this as a very real danger. This extraordinary purge, not only of the ruler's enemies, but of his bureaucracy — the transmission belts of his system — is, I think, unique in history, and is totally unlike the Stalinist terror. Mao made fools, in public, of the Mandarins, but then, instead of having their heads cut off, he put them back in office, and the people, having had the Mandarins guyed and seen through, will perhaps now not kowtow so abjectly as, according to tradition, they would be inclined to do. I think this was in Mao's mind.

URBAN If one could set aside the appalling cruelties that preceded (and partly also accompanied) the Cultural Revolution, one

92

might applaud, anyway, Mao's intention. I would personally rejoice at the thought of Italian bailiffs, French social security administrators, and even some British customs officers being given a taste of the Maoist whip.

TOYNBEE I think it would be a salutory exercise for all bureaucrats — they ought to be put through it at fairly short intervals.

You were drawing a parallel between the Pope's arbitral award in 1493 and the claim of the Chinese to be pretenders to the third world's leadership. This raises the question of the religious aspect of Maoism. I would say the religious aspect of Maoism is treating human beings as human beings, respecting the dignity of human nature, and not allowing the humble to be browbeaten by Mandarins. Mao was prepared to sacrifice a great deal of efficiency, and at some points even control of the situation, in order to save human freedom and the dignity of the human spirit. This is a religious element in Maoism which is not annulled by the fact that it was dressed up in the language of Confucio-Marxism and used as a tool of anti-Soviet propaganda.

*   *   *

URBAN I shall now turn to your concept of the "proletariat," for it bears a prophetic resemblance to what is popularly known as "alienation" today. In the fifth volume of your *Study,* where you examine the Hellenic prototype of internal proletariats, you say that "proletarianism is a state of feeling rather than a matter of outward circumstances," and earlier in your book you define the "proletariat" as a "social element or group which in some way is 'in' but not 'of' any given society. . . ." "The true hallmark of the proletarian," you write, "is neither poverty nor humble birth but a consciousness — and the resentment which this consciousness inspires — of being disinherited from his ancestral place in Society and being unwanted in a community which is his rightful home." If we apply your definition to modern conditions, your net catches a much larger section of society than does the Marxist definition, although I take it you would include the pauperized and alienated masses of industrial workers in your "internal proletariat."

TOYNBEE Yes, I would, as indeed I included the pauperized peasantry in my examination of Hellenic conditions, for example, the Italian peasantry, uprooted and impoverished as a consequence of the Hannibalic war.

URBAN Who then, apart from the fast diminishing class of industrial proletarians, belongs to the modern proletariats in your definition? Youth? The Negroes of the United States? Deraciné French Canadians? Czechs and Hungarians under Soviet rule?

TOYNBEE My definition sounds paradoxical. Take the case of Tolstoy: He was an aristocrat in his private life; he was privileged to do what he liked, to enjoy all the wealth he needed, to defy public opinion, and so on. But he was alienated from the Tsarist regime; he was one of the Russian intelligentsia who refused, in the period from 1825 onward, to serve as a tool and a creature of the Imperial regime. The Russian intelligentsia became opponents of the Imperial regime and managed to overthrow it, whereupon, ironically, they immediately became the establishment themselves.

Or take the case of South Africa. In South Africa the black majority is obviously a proletariat, but what about the smallish but very important white minority who are utterly up against apartheid and who feel they have been disinherited in the sense that they are carriers of the liberal traditions of the Western world, the traditions that have prevailed since the

close of the seventeenth century? These traditions are pro-
scribed in South Africa, and the minority who adhere to them
are actually persecuted. Aren't they part of the proletariat —
alongside of the blacks of South Africa? Many of this white
minority are eminent intellectuals, some of them are wealthy,
but from this spiritual and psychological point of view I think
they are part of the proletariat.

Then, in the Western world, people like the hippies, who are
rather typically the children of wealthy parents, are also part
of the proletariat. On the other hand, skilled workers who are
very effectively unionized and who earn high wages, are obviously part of the establishment now — they are, in fact,
arch-advocates of the system of free economic enterprise which
is the hallmark of capitalism. At the bottom of this industrial
ladder there is now only 5 per cent or 10 per cent, in a kind
of sump, who do not benefit from trade union strategy, who
cannot exert pressure and are very much left out. This residue
of unskilled and undereducated workers is very much a proletariat. The problem with these people is that they are a
penalized minority, not a majority, hence they are in the
weakest possible position. This is very apparent in America.
In a less affluent country this proletariat in the conventional
sense would be in a stronger position, for it would at least
have the advantage of numbers.

URBAN Left-wing social philosophers, like Herbert Marcuse, take a
very similar view, some hoping that these proletariats will
form a united revolutionary force to replace the revolutionary
working class in which the philosophers have lost confidence.
Can you see these groups crossing the barriers of cultural
background, race, and languages, sharing a philosophy and
acting together rather in the way in which Marxists hoped the
working class would?

TOYNBEE No, this seems very unlikely. As I say, the prosperous workers have become converts to the free enterprise, capitalist system, so any alliance between them and the alienated elements has to be ruled out. Can the poor whites and the Negroes at the bottom of the economic scale cooperate with the hippies who are at the top of the economic scale in the sense that they are probably the sons and daughters of well-to-do parents? This is going to be most difficult, and even if they could effectively combine, they would still be a minority. If I'm right in thinking that the so-called "blue-collar" workers have joined the middle class, then the bourgeoisie becomes crushingly strong. Add to this the unionization of the professional middle class — as, for instance, the civil servants are being unionized in this country — and the minority status of the proletariat is further accentuated. What I foresee is the unionization of various privileged groups: The representatives of civil servants, doctors, teachers might find that they are speaking the same language as the representatives of the engineers, electricity workers, the graphical society, etc. And if they combined together, they might be overwhelmingly more powerful than the rest of society, replacing, in fact, nationally elected governments with tyrannical minority rule. This is an alarming prospect.

URBAN Wouldn't this be generalizing from the British experience?

TOYNBEE I think Britain is certainly further advanced on this ruinous road than most industrialized Western countries, but other Western countries are moving in the same direction.

URBAN You show in your *Study* that the so-called higher religions — Christianity among them — arise, during the disintegration of civilizations, within the bosom of internal proletariats as a nonviolent expression of their estrangement from society. Some proletariats, you argue, reacted to their alienation violently, but others chose the path of gentleness, and spiritualized, so to speak, their misfortune into either "otherwordly" religions, such as Christianity, or into mundane nonviolence, such as Gandhiism, or yet again into some passive acceptance of God's plan for the world, such as the Jewish Diaspora's "Agudath Israel." Alienated minorities — and majorities — abound in the world today. Are these proletariats likely to generate higher forms of spiritual activity of the kind that would deserve to be called religions? There is no shortage of indications that the worship of a great assortment of private — and not so private — fancies is on the increase. But would they become religions?

TOYNBEE Probably they wouldn't; I see precious little sign of it at present. The people at the bottom of the scale in the United States have appealed to force. The Black Power adherents, after waiting patiently for a century after the abolition of slavery for genuine social, economic and cultural equality, have taken to violence. A tragic decision but, in America, this is the main discernible trend at the moment. The hippies — how seriously does one take the Jesus movement? It is a very crude form of revivalism — though it is certainly a symptom that mere negativism is not enough. So I don't see any encouraging symptoms of higher religions emerging again from the proletariat in my sense of the word proletariat.

URBAN The violence of the American Negroes must have struck you with special force because you are on record, in your *Study*, as saying that the Christianization of the American Negroes by their nominally Christian masters was accomplished rapidly and very thoroughly. You were saying, in fact, that these formerly savage Africans made exemplary Christians. All that is now gone: A great many American Negroes have reverted back to Africanism.

TOYNBEE When I first visited the United States I came across Negroes in ordinary life, especially in trains — Pullman cars, sleeping cars — where they served as attendants. I was enormously struck by their good humor, their humanity and kindness; I felt, now these people have been terribly treated, and yet they aren't embittered. But, I'm afraid, this has completely changed within my lifetime, and when I meet Negroes in America now, I get a different impression of their state of mind.

URBAN So the success of the conversion of these Negroes has worn off.

TOYNBEE Yes, because the nominally Christian Protestant establishment has not responded — they have not said, "We are all fellow-Christians, this is a human bond between us" and acted accordingly. In Mexico the history of Christianity in the relation between the conqueror and the conquered has been happier. The conquered were converted to Catholicism, and in the very first generation of the Spanish conquest a miracle is said to have occurred to a native Mexican convert: The Virgin of Guadalupe — now the patron saint of Mexico — appeared to this Indian convert, with copper-colored skin and in Indian dress. This spontaneous assimilation of Christianity has been the real link between the races. In present-day Mexico, village life revolves entirely around some sixteenth or seventeenth century church, probably built by Franciscans. The villagers are quite unconscious of ever having been anything but Christians, and you will find them spending their spare time gilding the cherubs with which their churches are ornamented. The Mexican intelligentsia, on the other hand, which has much more white blood than the villagers, is self-consciously anti-Cortes, pre-Columbian, and very keen on upholding and reviving the indigenous culture that has been swamped by the conquerors. A strange reversal of roles.

URBAN The slaves imported by the Roman empire from Asia Minor and the shores of North Africa retained their religion. Some were Christians, others belonged to non-Christian religions. Why did this not happen in the Americas?

TOYNBEE There is a great difference here between the destinies of slaves brought to North America and of those brought to Latin America. Some of the slaves brought to North America were from the West Coast of Africa, where there was an appreciable degree of indigenous African civilization which is now being brought to light by African studies. In the United States and in the West Indies — i.e., in the white Protestant territories — the native culture of the slaves was simply effaced, whereas in Latin America it was not. The Latin American cultural history of the slaves is much more like the Roman history of the slaves — especially of those imported from the Levant — in that they not only retained their culture but they imparted it to some extent to their masters. In Brazil, for instance, as in Roman Italy, it was a two-way relation between slaves and masters — it was only a one-way process in the United States. In Brazil, the Africans retained enough of their African culture and religion to have a visible effect on their European-descended owners, with the result that in Brazil there are to this day Afro-Christian cults in which every cult object is both a Christian saint and an African god, and the fraternities which practice these cults include both Africans and Europeans and mestizos, who are between the two. In some parts of Brazil even the Yoruba language survives as the cult language of some of these rituals. None of this would be conceivable in the United States.

URBAN On that analogy, would you expect a new religion to emerge from the union of Marxism and one, or perhaps several, of the "proletarian religions" such as Maoism or some Latin American form of Christianity? We have already seen that the

99

"inner" proletariat — hippies, youth, lower paid white proletarians, American Negroes — are unlikely to make new spiritual discoveries. Mightn't the "external proletariat" — the Chinese, the Latin Americans, the underprivileged peoples of the Indian subcontinent, i.e., the poor majority of the world — etherialize their own suffering into a faith, or faiths, which the numerically declining proletariats of the West are unable to do, or are uninterested in doing?

TOYNBEE I think the present situation in some parts of Latin America, especially in Brazil, is very suggestive of this. You have great social inequalities and injustices — extreme degrees of poverty and wealth. You have an un-Brazilian, repressive, and authoritarian government rather like the one in Greece and, most interesting of all, in the Roman Catholic hierarchy, from the Archbishop of Olinda down to the parish priests, you have a very radical social movement in favor of the underdog. The present Brazilian regime is more terrified of the Archbishop than of anybody else.

URBAN Some of the Catholic clergy in Latin America are open Marxists as well as Christians.

TOYNBEE Yes, they are genuine Marxists and genuine Christians. Now, my opinion of Marxism is rather like yours — I think it is old-fashioned and fatally tied to a dogmatic reading of a particular, transient phase of social and economic life in nineteenth century Western Europe. So orthodox Marxism may not be the "wave of the future." We are coming back to a point we made earlier in this discussion where we tried to see whether Marxism had any answers to the problems of the individual, and we found that it had none. On this question of marrying Marxism to one of the "proletarian" creeds I would say there might very well be some marriage between the traditional, historic religions and some modern ideology in response to modern social and economic conditions. I don't think this will be, or need be, Marxism, and it will certainly not be orthodox Marxism, but we cannot exclude the possibility that, if social radicalism in one form or another and one of the higher religions were to run together, we might get something quite new which might be of value to the whole world.

URBAN Are you saying that your distinction between "internal" and "external" proletariats doesn't perhaps fully apply in the contemporary world?

TOYNBEE The "external" proletariat in my sense would be the so-called barbarians who were, historically, outside or on the fringes of civilization. The pressure of these barbarians was very important at a time when the geographical habitats of civilizations were just patches on the earth's surface and most of the human race was outside all the civilizations. Now that pressure has ceased. A few years ago the last "barbarians," the seasonal nomads in Afghanistan, Pakistan, and in the Soviet Union, were forcibly settled on the land by rather brutal methods. Thus the external proletariat in my sense is out; now that civilization has spread all over the habitable parts of the earth, the "barbarians" have been absorbed into the internal proletariat of the modern world.

The future of the third world — of the underdeveloped countries, of the partially but imperfectly or superficially Westernized countries — is the real question. In one sense they have become part of the internal proletariat because they have been drawn into the economic and technological global network of the modern Western world, and in that sense they are in the same position as the submerged tenth in, say, the United States. But suppose the line between the so-called developed countries and the so-called underdeveloped countries hardens, and it becomes obvious that the underdeveloped countries are never going to be able to do what Japan and Russia have done — that is, to raise themselves above the poverty line and become countries with apparently infinite possibilities of economic growth and expansion — what is going to be the relation of the third world to the affluent countries, including the Soviet Union and Japan? If the line is impassable, it may be that the third world will become a new "external" proletariat rather in the sense of Lin Piao. It will, in other words, fall into economic war and then open warfare with the privileged countries. You can already see this in Chile and the Arab countries: The first thing a revolutionary does is to confiscate United States investments or to raise the price of oil for the Western consumer. This may well go much further. Revolutionary governments in the third world will say: "These Westerners are wolfing up all the natural resources of the world; we have, fortunately for ourselves, a large part of the world's remaining reserves of copper and oil. We may not be able to develop these by ourselves at present, but neither are we going to let them be exploited by the neocolonialists. We will not be lured by Western cash — we'll keep our resources for ourselves and for the human race in general." Now, if this happens, the rich developed minority of mankind will find itself, first, in a state of economic siege, and then in a state of political and military siege. Much will depend on which way China goes.

If China chooses to give an example to the third world on the lines we have discussed — going some way toward industrialization but retaining a basically peasant way of life — the developing countries might follow suit, and in that case, from the point of view of the Western world (in which I include Russia and Japan), the third world might become an external proletariat, and this might mean global class-war between the besieged rich minority and the disinherited hungry majority of the human race.

*   *   *

URBAN I am impressed by the resilience of your sense of optimism, although I cannot share it. You have, I think, yourself said that Mussolini's, Stalin's, and Hitler's totalitarian rule, the rabid nationalism of almost the whole of Europe in the 1930s, and the Second World War did not vindicate the claim you had made in the first volume of your *Study* where you said, "The stage has ceased to be dominated by the Great Powers with their pretension to be universes in themselves." "In the new age," you wrote in 1932-33, "the dominant note in the corporate consciousness of communities is a sense of being parts of some larger universe, whereas, in the age which is now over, the dominant note in their consciousness was an aspiration to be universes to themselves."

Nevertheless, twelve volumes and a quarter of a century later, having examined the destruction and self-destruction of nations and civilizations through jealousy, pride, hatred, and ignorance, you express the view in the closing chapter of the last volume (*Reconsiderations*) of your *Study* that, slowly and gropingly, but nevertheless unmistakably, mankind is taking the first steps toward acquiring a sense of collective responsibility, and, with that, toward sainthood. This is coming very close to the theodicist's view that even in the teeth of manifest evil, divine providence is somehow triumphant.

If the first step on Man's road towards sainthood is the renunciation of Man's traditional role of being his brother's murderer, the second step would be an acceptance of Man's new role of being his brother's keeper; and, happily, this sense of responsibility for the positive welfare of Man's fellow human beings has already declared itself. . . . As landmarks in the advance of this modern humanitarianism, we may single out the abolition of the slave-trade and of slavery itself, the abolition of barbarous forms of punishment, the humanization of the treatment of prisoners and lunatics, the establishment of old-age pensions and national health services in general, the narrowing of the gulf between a poor majority's and a rich minority's conditions of life. This advance towards greater social justice through an increase in human kindness has been taking place in two fields simultaneously: as between different classes in a single country and also as between different countries in a world that is now in process of being unified morally and socially as well as technologically and militarily. . . . These practical steps towards the vindication of fundamental and universal human rights leave us still far away from the achievement of a communion of saints. Yet this conscious and deliberate advance towards brotherhood in a community embracing the whole human race is surely even farther removed from the involuntary sociality of the bee-hive and the ant-heap.

Now a dozen or more years have passed since those words were written, and we have already seen that you no longer subscribe to some of the sentiments you expressed in volume XII in 1960. There is, indeed, precious little in the record to make us feel that there has been an increase in human kindness in the world. Do the religious wars in Ireland and Pakistan attest to "Man's new role of being his brother's keeper," does the invasion and *Gleichschaltung* of Czechoslovakia, or torture in Algeria, South Africa, Vietnam, Greece, Brazil, or the mob trial and public execution of "class-enemies" in China, or the murder of a million Indonesian communists, or the mutilation and public display of thieves by President Bossaka's army-men, or genocide in Nigeria and the threat of genocide in the Middle East, or the expulsion of Asians by General Amin, or our enjoyment of cruelty, violence, and beastliness in all its forms? One could go on; I find our advance toward sainthood difficult to see. I fear it may rather be the case that we may even be losing the ground won by earlier generations. Is your optimism based on analysis, or is it a personal conviction?

TOYNBEE Probably personal conviction, but, as I have already said, in the last five or six years I have become definitely less optimistic. After each of the calamities — after the First and the Second World Wars — I thought: Well, now surely, surely we've learned a lesson from this — we shall not do it again. I still don't think we are going to have a third world war fought with atomic weapons, but I think we are already having the equivalent of a world war, taking it out on ourselves in various ways other than atomic warfare. We are in the middle of the next — a paroxysm of self-inflicted trouble. Its effect on us in terms of psychological upset and spiritual and moral disorientation is the equivalent of war.

Now the question is: Does this change my long-term view of human nature and its prospects? I would still say that I believe, on the whole, that in human nature the aspect of love will gain the upper hand over the aspects of greed and aggressiveness — but perhaps this is an open question. Perhaps my diminished optimism is due to age and length of experience — perhaps I am more cautious and more pessimistic simply because I'm eighty-three now instead of being seventy-three or sixty-three. Or it may be an objective judgement in the light of what has happened in recent years. Whatever the cause, I am definitely less optimistic than I was when I wrote *Reconsiderations*.

URBAN I would have thought it would be less difficult to be one's brother's keeper if there weren't so many brothers about. One can certainly not love a bus queue or a mob in a football stadium. When, in thirty years' time, the world's population is double its present number, our capacity to love our neighbors will be spread rather thin.

TOYNBEE This is a question of personal as opposed to impersonal, institutional relations. It is more difficult to behave inhumanely to a human being if you meet him personally. I have been told by combatants in the First World War that a soldier who had to kill personally, with a bayonet, had a terrible feeling, but he didn't feel this if he shot someone or blew up a group of enemy soldiers at a distance. This is irrational, but it makes my point. Also, in both world wars, the French and the British had nicknames for the Germans — if you called them Boches or Huns, you could kill them with a good conscience, they weren't human. If you thought of them as a young German called John or James with a letter in his pocket from his family, it was much harder to kill him with a happy conscience. Personal relations are, by nature, very restricted in numbers. Members of a family can know each other personally, so can inhabitants of a village; but already the citizens of even the smallest city-state in Greece or Sumeria were too numerous for all to know each other personally, and the same was true in Goethe's Weimar. Yet, in these small states or cities, the inhabitants shared in the same man-made environment — they had a lot of semipersonal relations. The scale of the city and the scale of society were small enough to make this possible. This is completely impossible in the present-day world. I suppose the citizens of San Marino or of the smaller Swiss cantons know each other personally, but this is an anachronism. There is no doubt that numbers cause depersonalization, and this in turn causes a decrease in humanitarianism. This is one of the maladies of the present world.

URBAN But if you live in a village or a small town, as I did when I was a child and a youth in Hungary, you soon discover that coziness breeds its own tyranny. You have no privacy, the social conventions are overpowering, and if you don't conform you're an outcast. Silone once described to me the even more vicious, Italian variant of this tyranny, so I began to understand why the Germans say *Stadtluft macht frei*.* At the same time I'm very conscious that, looking upon village life as I now do, from the city, city air does not make for freedom, and very probably it didn't in Goethe's time:

* City air makes you free.

Ich höre schon des Dorfs Getümmel,
Hier ist des Volkes wahre Himmel,
Zufrieden jauchzet gross und klein:
"Hier bin ich Mensch, hier darf
                              ichs sein!"

TOYNBEE   *Stadtluft macht frei?* When a villager is in bondage to a feudal lord he is definitely underprivileged; politically and economically he is unfree, and in this sense he leads a dehumanized life by our standards. On the other hand, all the villagers knew each other — they enjoyed the intimacy and solidarity of an enlarged family. The walled city was certainly a refuge against the economic and political unfreedom of feudalism, and in this sense *Stadtluft macht frei* was true, and it was also true that the peasant who had moved from a village to a city would miss the close personal life of the village — he would feel uprooted. On the other hand he would be delighted to get rid of the feudal lord; he would become apprenticed in a guild instead, and he would feel this was an enlargement of his liberty.

But when you come to industrialization, the balance of freedom changes very abruptly. Around the year 1800 the village handloom worker in England was forced to become an urban factory worker: I don't think the city air made him feel freer; already it was an enslavement and impoverishment of life, and this was to get much worse as the century wore on.

URBAN   The sad thing is that the criticism of the conception of man as an economic unit rather than a human personality (a conception which accounted for England's industrial success) was instantaneous, but no one listened to it at the time and, in fact, no one paid much attention to it until industrialization threatened to ruin our habitat a century and a half later.

That the dogmatic analysis of Marx and Engels went unheeded in England in the mid-nineteenth century is perhaps not surprising. But more popular voices were also raised: Carlyle, George Eliot, de Tocqueville, Henry Morley, Dickens, Ruskin. Yet they were brushed aside as sentimental philanthropy. They were accused, as, for instance, by Walter Bagehot, of making "men dissatisfied with their inevitable condition," of making them imagine that "its irremediable evils can be remedied." No lessons were learnt.

TOYNBEE This nonlearning from patent facts—this obstinate and persistent nonlearning makes me pessimistic. I'm coming back to this point because it does bear repeating. The facts that made me optimistic in the early '30s were genuine facts, and they survived even the disasters of Hitlerism and the Second World War, and they should be still relevant today. But the power of blinding ourselves to patent facts seems to be almost insuperable. Take, for example, the renewed accentuation of nationalism in an age when the whole economic and technological organization of the world is pointing toward global cooperation and integration. It is this wilful ignorance, so to speak, of the lessons of the past that depresses me.

URBAN You've been accused of taking insufficient account of nationalism in your *Study*.

TOYNBEE Yes, one shouldn't minimize the reality of a force that one opposes — there is always a temptation to try to think it away. As far as I have done that, I'm sure I have been mistaken. Nationalism — recently I have repeatedly said this — is still the most powerful ideology in the world at present. In America, for instance, you have conscription, absolutely contrary to the American way of life in the traditional sense. Yet, in the Civil War, and in both World Wars, the Americans allowed conscription for the sake of nationalism. If you look at Africa, you find that the mistakes and tragedies of European nationalism are being repeated there in very crude forms. "The Westerners are very powerful," the Africans may argue, "they conquered and dominated us militarily and culturally. Nationalism was their way of life, therefore nationalism must have been the secret of their power — therefore let's be nationalists and we shall be very powerful like them." This kind of thinking just bristles with logical fallacies, but it would explain why the Africans have become so uncritically nationalist. They haven't realized the fatal effect of nationalism on Western civilization. They have thought of it as a talisman of power. They don't understand what they're doing when they adopt Western ideas or try to imitate Western nations. This is a terrible comment on human nature — it is part of the difficulty we have discussed in another context: the difficulty of learning from other people's experience which we can see in the way children react to their parents. They don't learn from their parents' experience; if anything, they react against it. Now, this is serious because human culture, the fact of being human, depends on handing down a cultural tradition from one generation to another. If we are so recalcitrant by nature to learning from the experience of other people and earlier generations, our situation doesn't look promising.

*   *   *

URBAN Have you been able to distil any lasting lessons from your life-experience that you would want to pass on to future generations?

TOYNBEE Well, Goethe says,

Alles vergängliche ist nur ein Gleichnis

I suppose my life, too, is a metaphor — a metaphor of the fragility and precariousness of human life. I was named after an uncle of mine, Arnold Toynbee, whom I have never known and who died of meningitis at the age of thirty, leaving one book which was published posthumously from lecture notes. If I had died at his age, I should have died obscure and without achievement. I have always been conscious of early death, and the longer I have lived the more conscious I have been of my own unearned bonus of longevity. If I had been a combatant in the First World War, I might have been killed like so many of my school-fellows, and so many Germans, Austrians, and Hungarians on the other side. But for the accident of staying alive, I couldn't have done any of what I have done. I often think of what would have been achieved by my contemporaries who were killed at the age of twenty-five or twenty-six. The fact that any achievement one has made is due to chance, as well as to one's own ability and merit, is a very humbling and wholesome experience. I feel the loss of my contemporaries more and more every year that's added to my own life, because I feel the difference between their fate and mine, and how utterly unreasonable and irrational and barbarous it is that they should have perished.

The second aspect of my metaphor would be the importance of the transmutation of suffering. I have had my personal sufferings and, of course, public sufferings too, and if I had had a choice of not having those sufferings, I suppose I would have chosen not to have them. But having had them, the vital question is: What do you make of them? Do you simply take a negative attitude toward them, are you just embittered by them or crushed by them, or are you able to make something of yourself through them? I have tried to do that. All human efforts are imperfect, but, as far as I have done that, I believe I have met my suffering in the right way. Shakespeare says (in *Richard II*) "They breathe truth that breathe their words in pain," and there is the famous passage in *Faust* where God says to Mephistopheles:

Des Menschen Tätigkeit kann allzu leicht erschlaffen,
Er liebt sich bald die unbedingte Ruh;

Drum geb ich gern ihm den Gesellen zu,
Der reizt und wirkt und muss als Teufel schaffen.

Der reizt und wirkt und muss als Teufel schaffen — I think
it is a profound truth about human life that the devil is a
necessary irritator or provoker; he's a piece of grit that creates
the pearl in the oyster, though it's nasty for the oyster. But
the pearl is a thing of beauty and value in itself. This is one
of the conditions of human life — it has been put in many
ways by people who saw to the bottom of things. It has been
put in two words by Aeschylus: *pathei mathos* — learning
from suffering, you must have suffering in order to learn. We
touched on this before, when we discussed the birth of civilizations under the impact of hard physical and psychic conditions.

URBAN One of the tragedies of life is summed up in the biblical
phrase: Many are called but few are chosen. You belong to
that small band of people who are exceptionally able, exceptionally articulate, and exceptionally successful. Mass education has increased the poignancy of the biblical phrase: For
every articulate historian, every poet, and every artist there
are thousands of able and sensitive people who have suffered,
who are burning inside but who haven't the power to be articulate. Higher education has implanted in them the desire, but
hasn't given them the ability, to be so. Some of the "counter-
culture" of our day feeds on these tragic frustrations.

TOYNBEE I get pathetic letters from people saying: I have a manuscript
on the meaning of history — Toynbee kind of stuff — but I
can't get a publisher to take it, can you help me? And often I
can see why the publisher won't take it. Yes, few are chosen
— this is the tragedy of life, and if one has success, one feels
very rueful about people who haven't. People who have lived
to have a try and not had success are more tragic than those,

like my uncle or my contemporaries in the First World War, who were destroyed by some external force.

URBAN How important is it to be articulate? Articulation releases tension and soothes suffering, but wouldn't an entirely introverted Arnold Toynbee, who has never set pen to paper, be just as dear in the sight of God as the writer of *A Study of History*? Or is there something in the act of naming things that adds to our spiritual estate?

TOYNBEE The worth of a blind and paralyzed painter who has never dipped a brush in paint would be no less than if he were articulate. I do believe that there is an absolute value in the human spirit quite apart from its material effects on society. There are many such people in the world. They would probably say — if they were religious — that their emotional and spiritual life was between them and God, that living and working in the sight of God was sufficient for them; they didn't need their fellow men. Would this impoverish the spiritual estate of man? Yes, I think it would, not only because the estate of man is poorer for not having these people being articulate, but also because they had some unique and priceless quality to give which they have, in fact, not given.

URBAN Would you have opted, in a less secular age, for a saintly and monastic life?

TOYNBEE Yes, perhaps I might have joined some learned monastic order if I had been a Westerner in the Middle Ages. What my experience would have been, I don't know. Would I have been an orthodox, or would I have been a heretic and have got into trouble over that? I was brought up as a conventional Anglican. I dropped out of this at the university. There then developed in me a seemingly unorthodox and unconventional, but for me very genuine, form of religion which has stayed with me as a vital charge all my life. It is an inner feeling, without the outward structure of religion.

URBAN It doesn't speak for orthodoxy. You end your *Study* with a syncretic prayer to Jesus Christ and the prophets and saints of all higher religions: "Christ Tammuz, Christ Adonis, Christ Osiris, Christ Balder, hear us, by whatsoever name we bless Thee for suffering death for our salvation." This is the voice of mysticism aspiring to the condition of sainthood.

TOYNBEE It is the voice of a historian who believes that, through the frame of history, God reveals himself, dimly and partially, to people who are sincerely seeking him. *Quot homines, tot sententiae:* each must speak for himself.